BILLI(

THE BANKER$

DEBTS FOR THE

PEOPLE

Reprint of Sheldon Emry's 1984 Booklet
Plus
Additions by author Larry Flinchpaugh

By:
J L Flinchpaugh Publishing Company
5500 Cape Court
St. Joseph, Missouri 64503
March 1, 2012
April 16, 2013

lflinch@stjoelive.com
www.larryflinchpaugh.com

ISBN-13: 978-0615623269
ISBN-10: 0615623263

Introduction

By J. Larry Flinchpaugh

The following expose on the corrupt monetary system the bankers have foisted upon the American people is incredible but true.

Part One is a reprint of Sheldon Emry's book, **"BILLION$ FOR THE BANKER$-DEBTS FOR THE PEOPLE"** concerning the international bankers and the unconstitutional privately owned Federal Reserve System that, since 1913, has looted the citizens out of trillions of dollars. It was published without any copyright so it could be easily and economically distributed world wide. Mr. Emry clearly explains the simplicity yet evilness of the "Banksters" great scam against us. Although written in 1984, the same principles still apply.

Part Two © Elaborates on this important work with comments and additional information by author Larry Flinchpaugh concerning the Money-Control over America.

Part Three © "Credit As a Public Utility"

Part Four © "Flinchpaugh Gazette".

The first step in fixing our country's flawed monetary system is to educate the public so they will elect representatives who will vote to abolish the privately owned *"Federal Reserve"* that charges the taxpayer unnecessary interest for loaning them their own money. Then allow the U.S. Treasury Department to print our money "interest free" as provided for in the Constitution. Secondly, *"Fractional Reserve Banking"* should only be allowed to state banks owned by the state (taxpayer).

For additional copies mail $6.00 each to cover printing costs and shipping and handling to: J L Flinchpaugh Publishing Company 5500 Cape Court St. Joseph, Mo. 64503

Or

order from Amazon.com

-Part One-
Introduction
BILLIONS FOR THE BANKERS-DEBTS FOR THE PEOPLE
By Sheldon Emry

In 1901 the national debt of the United States was less than $1 billion. It stayed at less than $1 billion until we got into World War I; then it jumped to $25 billion.

The national debt nearly doubled between World War I and World War II, increasing from $25 to $49 billion.

Between 1942 and 1952, the debt zoomed from $72 billion to $265 billion. In 1962 it was $303 billion. By 1970, the debt had increased to $383 billion.

Between 1971 and 1976 it rose from $409 billion to $631 billion. The debt experienced its greatest growth, however, during the 1980s, fueled by an unprecedented peacetime military buildup. In 1998, the outstanding public debt will roar past $5.5 trillion.

The unconstitutional "share" of this debt for every man, woman and child is currently $20,594.86 *(August 2011 it is $46,790)* and will continue to increase an average of $630 million every day, which doesn't include the $26 trillion in individual credit card debts, mortgages, automobile leases and so on.

U.S. NATIONAL DEBT the Outstanding Public Debt as of 08/25/98 at 10:28:37 AM PDT is: $5,516,699,306,752.93

Note: In 2012 the national debt is in excess of $15 trillion dollars.

Today, as we stand before the dawn of a **New World Order** run by internationalist financiers, most of the revenue collected by the Federal government in the form of individual income taxes will go straight to paying the interest on the debt alone. At the rate the debt is increasing, eventually we'll reach a point where, even if the government takes every penny of its citizens' income via taxation, it will still not collect enough to keep up with the interest payments.

The government will own nothing, the people will own nothing, and the banks will own everything. The New World Order will foreclose on America.

If the present trend continues, and there is no evidence whatsoever that it will not continue, we can expect the national debt to nearly double again within the next six to eight years. By then, the interest on the debt alone should be in the $400 billion a year range.

The love of money is the root of all evil." (1 Tim. 6:10) "If thou lend money to any of my people that is poor by thee, thou shalt not be to him as a usurer, neither shalt thou lay upon him usury." **Exodus 22:25**

"Take no usury of him, or increase...thou shalt not give him thy money upon usury." **Leviticus 25:36-67**

"Unto thy brother thou shalt not lend upon usury: That the Lord thy God may bless thee." **Deuteronomy 23:20** *(Note: Isn't the Bible saying that it is acceptable for a Jew to charge interest to a Gentile but not a fellow Jew? King James Bible- "Unto a stranger thou mayest lend upon usury; but unto thy brother thou shalt not lend upon usury...."*

In the early Church, *(Christian)* any interest on debt was considered usury.

Three Types Of Conquest

History reveals nations can be conquered by the use of one or more of three methods. *The most common is conquest by war.* In time, though, this method usually fails, because the captives hate

iv

the captors and rise up and drive them out if they can. Much force is needed to maintain control, making it expensive for the conquering nation.

A second method is by religion, where men are convinced they must give their captors part of their earnings as "obedience to God." Such a captivity is vulnerable to philosophical exposure or by overthrow by armed force, since religion by its nature lacks military force to regain control, once its captives become "disillusioned."

The third method can be called economic conquest. It takes place when nations are placed under "tribute" without the use of visible force or coercion, so that the victims do not realize they have been conquered. "Tribute" is collected from them in the form of "legal" debts and taxes, and they believe they are paying it for their own good, for the good of others, or to protect all from some enemy. Their captors become their "benefactors" and "protectors." Although this is the slowest to impose, it is often quite long-lasting, as the captives do not see any military force arrayed against them, their religion is left more or less intact, they have freedom to speak and to travel, and they participate in "elections" for their rulers. Without realizing it, they are conquered, and the instruments of their own society are used to transfer their wealth to their captors and make the conquest complete. In 1900 the average American worker paid few taxes and had little debt.

Last year payments on debts and taxes took more than half of what he earned. Is it possible a form of conquest has been imposed on our people?

Read the following pages and decide for yourself. And may God have mercy on this once debt-free and great nation...
Sheldon Emry

BILLION$ FOR THE BANKER$
DEBTS FOR THE PEOPLE

The Real Story of the Money-Control Over America

Originally written by Sheldon Emry in 1984

This study on money *is not copyrighted*. It may be reproduced in whole or in part for the purpose of helping the American people.

"If the American people ever allow private banks to control the issue of their money, first by inflation and then by deflation, the banks and corporations that will grow up around them (around the banks), will deprive the people of their property until their children will wake up homeless on the continent their fathers conquered." Thomas Jefferson

---

Americans, living in what is called the richest nation on earth; seem always to be short of money. Wives are working in unprecedented numbers, husbands hope for overtime hours to earn more, or take part-time jobs evenings and weekends, children look for odd jobs for spending money, the family debt climbs higher, and psychologists say one of the biggest causes of family quarrels and breakups is "arguments over money." Much of this trouble can be traced to our present "debt-money" system. Too few Americans realize why our founding fathers wrote into Article I of the U.S. Constitution: Congress shall have the Power to Coin Money and Regulate the Value Thereof.

They did this, as we will show, in hopes it would prevent "love of money" from destroying the *Republic* they had founded. We shall see how subversion of Article I has brought upon us the "evil" of the Federal Reserve System and the 16th Amendment that allowed the government to collect income tax on people's wages.

Money is "Created", Not Grown or Built.

Economists use the term "create" when speaking of the process by which money comes into existence. "Creation" means making something which did not exist before. Lumber workers make boards from trees, workers build houses from lumber, and factories manufacture automobiles from metal, glass and other materials. But in all these they did not actually "create."

They only changed existing materials into a more usable and, therefore, more valuable form. This is not so with money. Here and here alone, man actually "creates" something out of nothing. A piece of paper of little value is printed so that it is worth a piece of lumber. With different figures it can buy the automobile or even the house. Its value has been "created" in the truest sense of the word.

"Creating" money is very profitable!

As is seen by the above, money is very cheap to make, and whoever does the "creating" of money in a nation can make a tremendous profit. Builders work hard to make a profit of 5 percent above their cost to build a house.

Auto makers sell their cars for 1 percent to 2 percent above the cost of manufacture and it is considered good business. But money "manufacturers" have no limit on their profits, since a few cents will print a $1 bill or a $10,000 bill.

2

That profit is part of our story, but first let's consider another unique characteristic of the thing -- money, the love of which is the "root of all evil".

Adequate money supply needed

An adequate supply of money is indispensable to civilized society. We could forego many other things, but without money industry would grind to a halt, farms would become only self-sustaining units, surplus food would disappear, jobs requiring the work of more than one man or one family would remain undone, shipping and large movement of goods would cease, hungry people would plunder and kill to remain alive, and all government except family or tribe would cease to function.

An overstatement, you say? Not at all. Money is the blood of civilized society, the means of all commercial trade except simple barter. It is the measure and the instrument by which one product is sold and another purchased. Remove money or even reduce the supply below that which is necessary to carry on current levels of trade, and the results are catastrophic.

For an example, we need only look at America's depression of the early 1930's.

Bankers' Depression of the 1930's.

In 1930 America did not lack industrial capacity, fertile farmlands, skilled and willing workers or industrious families. It had an extensive and efficient transportation system in railroads, road networks, and inland and ocean waterways. Communications between regions and localities were the best in the world, utilizing telephone, teletype, radio, and a well operated government mail system.

No war had ravaged the cities or the countryside, no pestilence weakened the population, nor had famine stalked the land. The United States of America in 1930 lacked only one thing: an adequate supply of money to carry on trade and commerce.

3

In the early 1930s, bankers, the only source of new money and credit, deliberately refused loans to industries, stores and farms. Payments on existing loans were required however, and money rapidly disappeared from circulation. Goods were available to be purchased, jobs waiting to be done, but the lack of money brought the nation to a standstill.

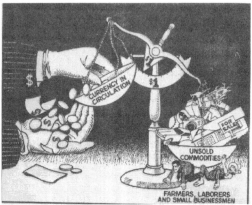

By this simple ploy America was put into a "depression" and bankers took possession of hundreds of thousands of farms, homes, and business properties. The people were told, "times are hard" and "money is short." Not understanding the system, they were cruelly robbed of their earnings, their savings, and their property.

No Money for Peace, but Plenty for War.

World War II ended the "depression." The same Bankers who in the early 1930's had no loans for peacetime houses, food and clothing, suddenly had unlimited billions to lend for army barracks, K-rations and uniforms.

A nation that in 1934 could not produce food for sale, suddenly could produce bombs to send free to Germany and Japan! (More on this riddle later).

With the sudden increase in money, people were hired, farms sold their produce, factories went to two shifts, mines reopened, and "The Great Depression" was over!

Some politicians were blamed for it and others took credit for ending it. The truth is the lack of money (caused by Bankers) brought on the depression, and adequate money ended it. The people were never told that simple truth and in this article we will endeavor to show how these same bankers who control our money and credit have used their control to plunder America and place us in bondage.

Power to Coin and Regulate Money

When we can see the disastrous results of an artificially created shortage of money, we can better understand why our Founding Fathers, who understood both money and God's Laws, insisted on placing the power to "create" money and the power to control it ONLY in the hands of the Federal Congress. They believed that ALL Citizens should share in the profits of its "creation" and therefore the Federal government must be the only creator of money. They further believed that all citizens, of whatever state, territory or station in life, would benefit by an adequate and stable currency. Therefore, the Federal government must also be, by law, the only controller of the value of money.

Since the Federal Congress was the only legislative body subject to all the citizens at the ballot box, it was, to their minds, the only safe depository of so much profit and so much power. They wrote it out in simple, but all inclusive manner: "Congress shall have the power to Coin Money and Regulate the Value Thereof."

How We Lost Control of the Federal Reserve

Instead of the Constitutional method of creating our money and putting it into circulation, we now have an entirely *unconstitutional* system. This has brought our country to the brink of disaster, as we shall see. Since our money was handled both legally and illegally before 1913, we shall consider only the years following 1913, since from that year on, all of our money had been created and issued by an illegal method that will eventually destroy the United States if it is not changed. Prior to 1913, America was a prosperous, powerful, and growing nation, at peace with its neighbors and the envy of the world. But in December of

1913, Congress, with many members away for the Christmas Holidays, passed what has since been known as the Federal Reserve Act. For the full story of how this infamous legislation was forced through our Congress, read "*Conquest or Consent*", by W. D. Vennard and "*The Creature from Jekyll Island* by G. Edward Griffin.

Omitting the burdensome details, it simply authorized the establishment of a Federal Reserve Corporation, run by a Board of Directors (The Federal Reserve Board). The act divided the United States into 12 Federal Reserve "Districts." This simple, but terrible, law completely removed from Congress the right to "create" money or to have any control over its "creation", and gave that function to The Federal Reserve Corporation. It was accompanied by the appropriate fanfare. The propaganda claimed that this would "remove money from politics" (they did not say "and therefore from the people's control") and prevent "boom and bust" economic activity from hurting our citizens.

The people were not told then, and most still do not know today, that the Federal Reserve Corporation is a *private* corporation controlled by bankers and therefore is operated for the financial gain of the bankers over the people rather than for the good of the people. The word *"Federal"* was used only to deceive the people.

More Disastrous than Pearl Harbor

Since that "day of infamy", more disastrous to us than Pearl Harbor, the small group of "privileged" people who lend us "our" money have accrued to themselves all of the profits of printing our money -- and more! Since 1913 they have "created" tens of billions of dollars in money and credit, which, as their own personal property, they can lend to our government and our people at interest (usury).

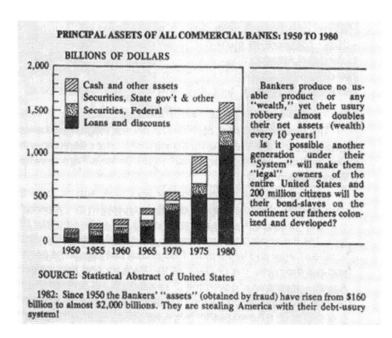

PRINCIPAL ASSETS OF ALL COMMERCIAL BANKS: 1950 TO 1980

BILLIONS OF DOLLARS

Cash and other assets
Securities, State gov't & other
Securities, Federal
Loans and discounts

Bankers produce no usable product or any "wealth," yet their usury robbery almost doubles their net assets (wealth) every 10 years! Is it possible another generation under their "System" will make them "legal" owners of the entire United States and 200 million citizens will be their bond-slaves on the continent our fathers colonized and developed?

1950 1955 1960 1965 1970 1975 1980

SOURCE: Statistical Abstract of United States

1982: Since 1950 the Bankers' "assets" (obtained by fraud) have risen from $160 billion to almost $2,000 billions. They are stealing America with their debt-usury system!

"The rich get richer and the poor get poorer" had become the secret policy of the Federal government. An example of the process of "creation" and its conversion to peoples "debt" will aid our understanding.

Billions in Interest Owed to Private Banks

We shall start with the need for money. The Federal Government, having spent more than it has taken from its citizens in taxes, needs, for the sake of illustration, $1,000,000,000. Since it does not have the money, and Congress has given away its authority to "create" it, the Government must go to the "creators" for the $1 billion.

But, the Federal Reserve, a private corporation, does not just give its money away! The Bankers are willing to deliver $1,000,000,000 in money or credit to the Federal Government in exchange for the government's agreement to pay it back -- with interest. So Congress authorizes the Treasury Department to print $1,000,000,000 in U.S. Bonds, which are then delivered to the Federal Reserve Bankers.

7

The Federal Reserve then pays the cost of printing the $1 billion (about $1,000) and makes the exchange. *The privately owned Federal Reserve actually created this money out of thin air!* The government then uses the money to pay its obligations. What are the results of this fantastic transaction? Well, $1 billion in government bills are paid all right, but the Government has now indebted the people to the bankers for $1 billion on which the people must pay interest!

Tens of thousands of such transactions have taken place since 1913 so that in 1996, the U.S. Government is indebted to the Bankers for more than $5,000,000,000,000 (trillion). Most of the income taxes that we pay as individuals now goes straight into the hands of the bankers, just to pay off the interest alone, with no hope of ever paying off the principle. Our children will be forced into servitude.

But wait! There's more!

You say, "This is terrible!" Yes, it is, but we have shown only part of the sordid story. Under this unholy system, those United States Bonds have now become "assets" of the banks in the Reserve System which they then use as "reserves" to *"create" more "credit"* to lend. Current "reserve" requirements allow them to use that $1 billion in bonds to "create" as much as $15 billion in new "credit" to lend to states, municipalities, to individuals and businesses.

Added to the original $1 billion, they could have $16 billion of "created credit" out in loans paying them interest with their only cost being $1,000 for printing the original $1 billion! Since the U.S. Congress has not issued Constitutional money since 1863 (more than 100 years), in order for the people to have money to carry on trade and commerce they are forced to borrow the "created credit" of the Monopoly bankers and pay them usury-interest!

Manipulating Stocks for Fun and Profit

In addition to almost unlimited usury, the bankers have another method of drawing vast amounts of wealth. The banks who control the money at the top are able to approve or disapprove large loans to large and successful corporations to the extent that refusal of a loan will bring about a reduction in the selling price of the corporation's stock.

After depressing the price, the bankers' agents buy large blocks of the company's stock. Then, if the bank suddenly approves a multi-million dollar loan to the company, the stock rises and is then sold for a profit. In this manner, billions of dollars are made with which to buy more stock. This practice is so refined today that the Federal Reserve Board need only announce to the newspapers an increase or decrease in their "discount rate" to send stocks soaring or crashing at their whim.

Using this method since 1913, the bankers and their agents have purchased secret or open control of almost every large corporation

9

in America. Using this leverage, they then force the corporations to borrow huge sums from their banks so that corporate earnings are siphoned off in the form of interest to the banks. This leaves little as actual "profits" which can be paid as dividends and explains why banks can reap billions in interest from corporate loans even when stock prices are depressed. In effect, the bankers get a huge chunk of the profits, while individual stockholders are left holding the bag.

The millions of working families of America are now indebted to the few thousand banking families for twice the assessed value of the entire United States. And these Banking families obtained that debt against us for the cost of paper, ink, and bookkeeping!

The interest amount is never created
The only way new money (which is not true money, but rather credit representing a debt), goes into circulation in America is when it is borrowed from the bankers. When the State and people borrow large sums, we seem to prosper. However, the bankers "create" only the amount of the principal of each loan, never the extra amount needed to pay the interest. Therefore, the new money never equals the new debt added. The amounts needed to pay the interest on loans is not "created," and therefore does not exist!

Under this system, where new debt always exceeds new money no matter how much or how little is borrowed, the total debt increasingly outstrips the amount of money available to pay the debt. The people can never, ever get out of debt!

The following example will show the viciousness of this interest-debt system via its "built in" shortage of money.

The Tyranny of Compound Interest
When a citizen goes to a banker to borrow $100,000 to purchase a home or a farm, the bank clerk has the borrower agree to pay back

the loan plus interest. At 8.25% interest for 30 years, the borrower must agree to pay $751.27 per month for a total of $270,456.00.

The clerk then requires the citizen to assign to the banker the right of ownership of the property if the borrower does not make the required payments. The bank clerk then gives the borrower a $100,000 check or a $100,000 deposit slip, crediting the borrower's checking account with $100,000.

The borrower then writes checks to the builder, subcontractors, etc. who in turn write checks. $100,000 of new "checkbook" money is thereby added to the "money in circulation."

However, this is the fatal flaw in the system: the only new money created and put into circulation is the amount of the loan, $100,000. The money to pay the interest is NOT created, and therefore was NOT added to "money in circulation."

Even so, this borrower (and those who follow him in ownership of the property) must earn and take out of circulation $270,456.00, $170,456.00 more than he put in circulation when he borrowed the original $100,000! (This interest cheats all families out of nicer homes. It is not that they cannot afford them; it is because the bankers' interest forces them to pay for nearly 3 homes to get one!)

Every new loan puts the same process in operation. Each borrower adds a small sum to the total money supply when he borrows, but the payments on the loan (because of interest) then deduct a much larger sum from the total money supply.

There is therefore no way all debtors can pay off the money lenders. As they pay the principle and interest, the money in circulation disappears. All they can do is struggle against each other, borrowing more and more from the money lenders each generation. The money lenders (bankers), who produce nothing of value, gradually gain a death grip on the land, buildings, and present and future earnings of the whole working population.

Proverbs 22:7 has come to pass in America. "The rich ruleth over the poor, and the borrower is servant to the lender."

Small loans do the same thing

If you have not quite grasped the impact of the above, let us consider an auto loan for 5 years at 9.5% interest. Step 1: Citizen borrows $25,000 and pays it into circulation (it goes to the dealer, factory, miner, etc.) and signs a note agreeing to pay the Bankers a total of $31,503 over 5 years. Step 2: Citizen pays $525.05 per month of his earnings to the Banker. In five years, he will remove from circulation $6,503 more than he put in circulation.

Every loan of banker "created" money (credit) causes the same thing to happen. Since this has happened millions of times since 1913 (and continues today), you can see why America has gone from a prosperous, debt-free nation to a debt-ridden nation where practically every home, farm and business is paying usury-tribute to the bankers.

Checking Up On Cash

In the millions of transactions made each year like those just discussed, little actual currency changes hands, nor is it necessary that it do so.

About 95 percent of all "cash" transactions in the U. S. are executed by check. Consider also that banks must only hold 10 percent of their deposits on site in cash at any given time. This means 90 percent of all deposits, though they may actually be held by the bank, are not present in the form of actual cash currency.

That leaves the banker relatively safe to "create" that so-called "loan" by writing the check or deposit slip not against actual money, but against your promise to pay it back! The cost to him is paper, ink and a few dollars of overhead for each transaction. It is "check kiting" on an enormous scale. The profits increase rapidly, year after year.

12

Our Own Debt is Spiraling into Infinity

In 1910 the U. S. Federal debt was only $1 billion, or $12.40 per citizen. State and local debts were practically non-existent.

By 1920, after only six years of Federal Reserve shenanigans, the Federal debt had jumped to $24 billion, or $228 per person.

In 1960 the Federal debt reached $284 billion, or $1,575 per citizen and state and local debts were mushrooming.

In 1998 the Federal debt passed $5.5 trillion, or $20,403.90 per man, woman and child and is growing exponentially. *Note: $15 Trillion in 2012*

State and local debts are forever increasing. However, the banksters are too cunning to take the title to everything at once. They instead leave us with some "illusion of ownership" so you and your children will continue to work and pay the bankers more of your earnings on ever increasing debts. The "establishment" has captured our people with their debt-money system as certainly as if they had marched in with a uniformed army.

Gambling Away the American Dream

To grasp the truth that periodic withdrawal of money through interest payments will inexorably transfer all wealth in the nation to the receiver of interest, imagine yourself in a poker or dice game where everyone must buy the chips (the medium of exchange) from a "banker" who does not risk chips in the game.

He just watches the table and reaches in every hour to take 10 percent to 15 percent of all the chips on the table. As the game goes on, the amount of chips in the possession of each player will fluctuate according to his luck.

However, the total number of chips available to play the game (carry on trade and business) will decrease steadily.

As the game starts getting low on chips, some players will run out. If they want to continue to play, they must buy or borrow more chips from the "banker". The "banker" will sell (lend) them only if the player signs a "mortgage" agreeing to give the "Banker" some real property (car, home, farm, business, etc.) if he cannot make periodic payments to pay back all the chips plus some extra chips (interest). The payments must be made on time, whether he wins (makes a profit) or not.

It is easy to see that no matter how skillfully they play, eventually the "banker" will end up with all of his original chips back, and except for the very best players, the rest, if they stay in long enough, will lose to the "banker" their homes, their farms, their businesses, perhaps even their cars, watches, and the shirts off their backs!

Our real life situation is much worse than any poker game. In a poker game no one is forced into debt, and anyone can quit at any time and keep whatever he still has. But in real life, even if we borrow little ourselves from the "bankers," our local, State and Federal governments borrow billions in our name, squander it, then confiscate our earnings via taxation in order to pay off the bankers with interest.

We are forced to play the game, and none can leave except by death. We pay as long as we live, and our children pay after we die. If we cannot or refuse to pay, the government sends the police to take our property and give it to the bankers. The bankers risk nothing in the game; they just collect their percentage and "win it all." In Las Vegas, all games are rigged to pay the owner a percentage, and they rake in millions. The Federal Reserve bankers' "game" is also rigged, and it pays off in billions!

In recent years, Bankers have added some new cards to their deck: credit cards are promoted as a convenience and a great boon to trade. Actually, they are ingenious devices from the seller and 18% interest from buyers. A real "stacked" deck!

Yes, it's political too

Democrat, Republican, and independent voters who have wondered why politicians always spend more tax money than they take in should now see the reason. When they begin to study our money system, they soon realize that these politicians are not the agents of the people but are the agents of the bankers, for whom they plan ways to place the people further in debt.

It takes only a little imagination to see that if Congress had been "creating," spending and issuing into circulation the necessary increase in the money supply, there would be no national debt. Trillions of dollars of other debts would be practically non-existent.

Since there would be no original cost of money except printing, and no continuing costs such as interest, Federal taxes would be almost nil. Money, once in circulation, would remain there and go on serving its purpose as a medium of exchange for generation after generation and century after century, with no payments to the Bankers whatsoever!

Continuing Cycles of Debt and War

But instead of peace and debt-free prosperity, we have ever-mounting debt and cyclical periods of war. We as a people are now ruled by a system of banking influence that has usurped the mantle of government, disguised itself as our legitimate government, and set about to pauperize and control our people.

It is now a centralized, all-powerful political apparatus whose main purposes are promoting war, confiscating the people's money, and propagandizing to perpetuate its power. Our two main political parties have become its servants, the various departments of government have become its spending agencies, and the Internal Revenue Service is its collection agency.

Unknown to the people, it operates in close cooperation with similar apparatuses in other nations, which are also disguised as "governments."

Some, we are told, are friends. Some, we are told, are enemies. "Enemies" are built up through international manipulations and used to frighten the American people into going billions of dollars further into debt to the bankers for "military preparedness," "foreign aid to stop communism," "the drug war," etc.

Citizens, deliberately confused by brainwashing propaganda, watch helplessly while our politicians give food, goods, and money to banker-controlled alien governments under the guise of "better relations" and "easing tensions." Our banker-controlled government takes our finest and bravest sons and sends them into foreign wars where tens of thousands are murdered, and hundreds of thousands are crippled (not to mention collateral damage and casualties among the "enemy" troops.)

16

When the "war" is over, we have gained nothing, but we are billions of dollars further in debt to the bankers, which was the reason for the "war" in the first place!

And There's More

The profits from these massive debts have been used to erect a complete and, almost hidden, economic colossus, over our nation. They keep telling us they are trying to do us good, when in truth they work to bring harm and injury to our people. These would be despots know, it is easier to control and rob a ill, poorly educated, and confused people, than it is a healthy and intelligent population, so they deliberately prevent real cures for diseases, they degrade our educational systems, and they stir up social and racial unrest. For the same reason, they favor drug use, alcohol, sexual promiscuity, abortion, pornography, and crime. Everything, which debilitates the minds and bodies of the people, is secretly encouraged, as it makes the people less able to oppose them, or, even, to understand what is being done to them.

Family, morals, love of country, the Christian religion, all that is honorable, is being swept away, while they try to build their new, subservient man. Our new "rulers" are trying to change our whole racial, social, religious, and political order, but they will not change the debt-money-economic system, by which they rob and rule. Our people have become tenants and "debt-slaves", to the Bankers, and their agents, in the land our fathers conquered. It is conquest through the most, gigantic fraud and swindle, in the history of mankind. And we remind you again: The key to their wealth and power, over us, is their ability to create "money" out of nothing, and lend it to us, at interest. If they had not been allowed to do that, they would never have gained secret control of our nation. How true Solomon's words are: "The rich ruleth over the poor, and the borrower is servant to the lender "(Proverbs 22:7).

God Almighty warned, in the Bible, that one of the curses, which would come upon His people, for disobeying His laws was: The stranger that is within thee shall get up above thee very high; and

17

thou shall come down very low. He shall lend to thee, and thou shall not lend to him; he shall be the head, and thou shall be the tail. Deut. 28:44-45

Most of the owners of the large banks, in America, are of eastern-European ancestry, and connected with the Rothschild European banks. Has that warning come to fruition in America?

Let us, now, consider the *correct* method of providing the medium of exchange (money) needed by our people.

Every Citizen Can Be A Stock Holder in America
Under the Constitutional system, no private banks would exist to rob the people. Government banks under the control of the people's representatives would issue and control all money and credit. They would issue not only actual currency, but could lend limited credit at no interest for the purchase of capital goods, such as homes.

A $100,000 loan would require only $100,000 repayment, not $270,456.00 as it is now. Everyone who supplied materials and labor for the home would get paid just as they do today, but the bankers would not get $170,456.00 in interest.

That is why they ridicule and destroy anyone suggesting or proposing an alternative system.

18

History tells us of debt-free and interest-free money issued by governments.

The American colonies did it through colonial script in the 1700's. Their wealth soon rivaled that of England and brought restrictions from Parliament, which led to the Revolutionary War. Abraham Lincoln did it in 1863 to help finance the Civil War. He was later assassinated by a man many consider to have been an agent of the Rothschild Bank. No debt-free or interest-free money has been issued in America since then.

Several Arab nations issue interest free loans to their citizens today. *(Now you can understand what all the commotion in the Middle East is all about and why the banker-owned press is brainwashing American citizens to think of all Arabs as terrorists).* The Saracen Empire forbade interest on money 1,000 years ago and its wealth outshone even Saxon Europe. Mandarin China issued its own money, interest-free and debt-free. Today, historians and art collectors consider those centuries to be China's time of greatest wealth, culture and peace.

Issuing money which does not have to be paid back in interest leaves the money available to use in the exchange of goods and services and its only continuing cost is replacement as the paper wears out. *Money is the paper ticket by which transfers are made and should always be in sufficient quantity to transfer all possible production of the nation to the ultimate consumers.* It is as ridiculous for a nation to say to its citizens, "You must consume less because we are short of money," as it would be for an airline to say, "Our planes are flying, but we cannot take you because we are short of tickets".

CITIZEN CONTROL

Citizen Control of U.S. Currency

Money, issued in such a way, would derive its value in exchange from the fact that it had come from the highest legal source in the nation and would be declared legal to pay all public and private debts.

Issued by a sovereign nation, not in danger of collapse, it would need no gold or silver or other so-called "precious" metals to back it.

As history shows, the stability and responsibility of government issuing it is the deciding factor in the acceptance of that government's currency--not gold, silver, or iron buried in some hole in the ground. Proof is America's currency today. Our gold and silver is practically gone, but our currency is accepted. But if the government was about to collapse our currency would be worthless.

Under the present system, the extra burden of interest forces workers and businesses to demand more money for the work and goods to pay their ever increasing debts and taxes. This increase in prices and wages is called "inflation." Bankers, politicians and "economists" blame it on everything but the real cause, which is the interest levied on money and debt by the Bankers.

This "inflation" benefits the money-lenders, since it wipes out savings of one generation so they cannot finance or help the next generation, who must then borrow from the money-lenders and pay a large part of their life's labor to the usurer.

With an adequate supply of interest-free money, little borrowing would be required and prices would be established by people and goods, not by debts and usury.

Citizen Control

If the Congress failed to act, or acted wrongly in the supply of money, the citizens would use the ballot or recall petitions to replace those who prevented correct action with others whom the people believe would pursue a better money policy. *Since the creation of money and its issuance in sufficient quantity would be one of the few functions of Congress, the voter could decide on a candidate by his stand on money and other legitimate functions of the Federal government, instead of the diversionary issues which are presented to us today. All other problems, except the nation's defense, would be taken care of in the State, County, or City governments where they are best handled and most easily corrected.*

An adequate national defense would be provided by the same citizen- controlled Congress, and there would be no bankers behind the scenes, bribing politicians to spend billions of dollars on overseas military adventures which ultimately serve the schemes of international finance.

Creating a Debt-Free America

With debt-free and interest-free money, there would be no direct confiscatory taxation and our homes would be mortgage-free without approximately $10,000-per-year payments to the bankers. Nor would they get $1000 to $3000 per year from every automobile on our roads.

We would need far fewer financial "help" in the form of "easy payment" plans, "revolving" charge accounts, loans to pay medical or hospital bills, loans to pay taxes, loans to pay for burials, loans to pay loans, nor any of the thousand and one usury bearing loans which now suck the life blood of American families.

Our officials, at all levels of government, would be working for the people instead of devising capers which will place us further in debt to the bankers. *We would get out of entangling foreign alliances that have engulfed us in four major wars and scores of minor wars since the Federal Reserve Act was passed.*

A debt-free America would leave parents with more time to spend raising their children. *The elimination of the interest payments and debt would be the equivalent of a 50 percent raise in the purchasing power of every worker.* This cancellation of interest-based private debts would result in the return to the people of $300 billion yearly in property and wealth that currently goes to banks.

Controlling Public Debate and Opinion

We realize that this small, and necessarily incomplete, article on money may be charged with oversimplification. Some may say that if it is that simple the people would have known about it, and it could not have happened. But this conspiracy is as old as Babylon, and even in America it dates far back before the year 1913.

Actually, 1913 may be considered the year in which their previous plans came to fruition, opening the way for complete economic conquest of our people. The conspiracy is powerful enough in America to place its agents in positions as newspaper publishers, editors, columnists, church ministers, university presidents, professors, textbook writers, labor union leaders, filmmakers, radio and television commentators, politicians ranging from school board members to U. S. presidents, and many others.

These agents control the information available to our people. They manipulate public opinion, elect whomever they want locally and nationally, and *never expose the crooked money system*. They promote school bonds, expensive and detrimental farm programs, "urban renewal," foreign aid, and many other schemes which place the people more deeply in debt to the bankers.

Thoughtful citizens wonder why billions are spent on one program and billions on another which may duplicate it or even nullify it, such as paying some farmers not to raise crops, while at the same time building dams or canals to irrigate more farm land. Crazy or stupid?

Neither. The goal is more debt. Thousands of government-sponsored methods of wasting money go on continually. Most make no sense, but they are never exposed for what they really are: siphons sucking our Nation's economic lifeblood. Billions for the bankers, debts for the people.

Controlled news and information
So-called "economic experts" write syndicated columns in hundreds of newspapers, craftily designed to prevent the people from learning the simple truth about our money system.

Sometimes commentators, educators, and politicians blame our financial conundrum on the workers for being wasteful, lazy, or stingy. Other times, they blame workers and consumers for the increase in debts and the inflation of prices, when they know the cause is the debt-money system itself.

Our people are literally drowned in charges and counter-charges designed to confuse them and keep them from understanding the unconstitutional and evil money system that is so efficiently and silently robbing the farmers, the workers, and the businessmen of the fruits of their labor and of their freedoms. Some, who are especially vocal in their exposure of the treason against the people, are harassed by government agencies such as the EPA, OSHA, the

IRS, and others, forcing them into financial strain or bankruptcy. They have been completely successful in preventing most Americans from learning the things you have read in this article.

However, in spite of their control of information, they realize many citizens are learning the truth. (There are several millions

of Americans who now know the truth including former congressmen, former revenue agents, ministers, businessmen, and many others).

Therefore, to prevent armed resistance to their plunder of America, they plan to register all firearms and eventually to disarm all citizens, in violation of the 2nd Amendment to the Constitution of the United States of America. A people armed cannot be enslaved. Therefore, they only want guns in the hands of their government police or military forces--hands that are already stained with blood from countless acts of gross negligence and overt homicide, both at home and abroad.

Spread the Word and Do Something to Fix Things. The "almost hidden" conspirators in politics, religion, education, entertainment, and the news media are working for the banker-owned United States, in a banker-owned World under a banker-owned World Government! (This is what all the talk of a New World Order promoted by Presidents Bush and Clinton is all about.)

Unfair banking policies and taxes will continue to take a larger and larger part of the annual earning of the people and put them into the pockets of the bankers and their political agents. Increasing government regulations will prevent citizen protest and opposition to their control.

It is possible that your grandchildren will own neither home nor car, but will live in "government owned" apartments and ride to work in "government owned" buses (both paying interest to the bankers), and be allowed to keep just enough of their earnings to buy a minimum of food and clothing while their rulers wallow in luxury. In Asia and Eastern Europe it is called "communism;" in America it is called "Democracy" and "Capitalism."

America will not shake off her Banker-controlled dictatorship as long as the people are ignorant of the hidden controllers. Banking concerns, which control most of the governments of the nations, and most sources of information, seem to have us completely within their grasp. They are afraid of only one thing: an awakened patriotic citizenry, armed with the truth, and with a trust in God for deliverance. This material has informed you about their iniquitous system. What you do with it is in your hands.

WHAT YOU CAN DO

Pray for America's release from this wicked money control, which is at the root of our debts and wars.

Send copies of this article to officials in your State and Local government, to school board members, principals, teachers, ministers, neighbors, etc. Ask them for their comments.

25

Write letters to elected or appointed officials. Write "letters- to-the-editor" to newspapers. Most small towns and suburban newspapers are not totally controlled, while most of the big city newspapers are.

Give or mail them out by the hundreds to awaken and educate other Americans to this fantastic plunder of the working people of America. The cost to you is VERY LITTLE compared to the BILLIONS in money and property being STOLEN from our people.

QUOTES - FROM PROMINENT PEOPLE

VOLTAIRE (1694-1778)
"Paper money eventually returns to its intrinsic value ---- zero."

PRESIDENT JAMES A. GARFIELD

"Whoever controls the volume of money in any country is absolute master of all industry and commerce."

HORACE GREELY

"While boasting of our noble deeds, we are careful to control the ugly fact that by an iniquitous money system, we have nationalized a system of oppression which, though more refined, is not less cruel than the old system of chattel slavery."

SIR. REGINALD MCKENNA, former President of the Midland Bank of England

"Those who create and issue money and credit direct the policies of government and hold in the hollow of their hands the destiny of the people."

SIR JOSIAH STAMP, (President of the Bank of England in the 1920's, the second richest man in Britain)

"Banking was conceived in iniquity, and was born in sin. The Bankers own the Earth. Take it away from them, but leave them the power to create deposits, and with the flick of the pen, they will create enough deposits, to buy it back again. However, take it away from them, and all the great fortunes like mine will disappear, and they ought to disappear, for this would be a happier and better world to live in. But if you wish to remain the slaves of Bankers, and pay the cost of your own slavery, let them continue to create deposits."

ROTHSCHILDS BROS. OF LONDON

"Those few who can understand the system (check book money and credit) will either be so interested in its profits, or so dependent on it favors, that there will be little opposition from that class, while on the other hand, the great body of people mentally incapable of comprehending the tremendous advantage that capital derives from the system, will bear it burdens without complaint, and perhaps without even suspecting that the system is inimical to their interests."

ANSELM ROTHSCHILD

"Give me the power to issue a nation's money; then I do not care who makes the law."

PRESIDENT WOODROW WILSON

"A great industrial nation is controlled by its system of credit. Our system of credit is concentrated. The growth of the Nation and all our activities are in the hands of a few men. We have come to be one of the worst ruled, one of the most completely controlled and dominated governments in the world--no longer a government of free opinion, no longer a government of conviction, and vote of the majority, but a government by the opinion and duress, of small groups of dominant men."

Just before President Woodrow Wilson died, he is reported to have stated to friends that he had been "deceived" and that "I have betrayed my Country". Referring to the Federal Reserve Act, passed during his Presidency.

PELATIAH WEBSTER

"Paper money polluted the equity of our laws, turned them into engines of oppression, corrupted the justice of our public administration, destroyed the fortunes of thousands who had confidence in it, enervated the trade, husbandry, and manufactures of our country, and went far to destroy the morality of our people."

WILLIAM PATTERSON

"The bank hath benefit of interest on all moneys which it creates out of nothing."

POPE PIUS XI

"In the first place, then, it is patent that in our days, not wealth alone is accumulated, but immense power and despotic economic domination are concentrated in the hands of the few, who for the most part are not the owners but only the trustees and directors of invested funds, which they administer at their own good pleasure...This domination is most powerfully exercised by those who, because they hold and control money, also govern credit and determine its allotment, for that reason supplying so to speak, the life blood of the entire economic body, and grasping in their hands, as it were, the very soul of production, so that no one can breathe against their will..."

IRVING FISHER

"Thus, our national circulating medium is now at the mercy of loan transactions of banks, which lend, not money, but promises to supply money they do not possess."

MAJOR L. L. B. ANGUS

"The modern banking system manufactures money out of nothing. The process is, perhaps, the most, astounding piece of sleight of hand that was ever invented. Banks can in fact inflate, mint, and un-mint the modern ledger-entry currency".

RALPH M. HAWTREY
(Former Secretary of the British Treasury)

"Banks lend by creating credit. They create the means of payment, out of nothing."

ROBERT H. HEMPHILL (Credit Manager of Federal Reserve Bank, Atlanta, Georgia)

"This is a staggering thought. We are completely dependent, on the Commercial Banks. Someone has to borrow every dollar, we have in circulation, cash or credit. If the Banks create ample synthetic money, we are prosperous; if not, we starve. We are, absolutely, without a permanent money system. When one gets a complete grasp of the picture, the tragic absurdity, of our hopeless position, is almost incredible, but there it is. It is the most, important subject, intelligent persons can investigate and reflect upon. It is so important that our present civilization may collapse, unless it becomes widely understood, and the defects remedied very soon."

CONGRESSMAN LOUIS T. McFADDEN and former Chairman of the Committee on Banking and Currency.

"Mr. Chairman, we have in this country one of the most corrupt institutions the world has ever known. I refer to the Federal Reserve Board and the Federal Reserve Banks, hereinafter called the Fed. "The Federal Reserve (Banks) are one of the most corrupt institutions, the world has ever seen. There is not a man, within the sound of my voice, who does not know that this Nation is run by the International Bankers". This evil institution has impoverished and ruined the people of the United States. . . . Some people think the Federal Reserve Banks are United States Government institutions. They are private credit monopolies which prey upon the people of the United States for the Benefit of themselves and their foreign customers. ..."

The Fed has cheated the Government of the United States and the people of the United States out of enough money to pay the Nation's debt.... The wealth of these United States and the working capital have been taken away from them and has either been locked in the vaults of certain banks and the great corporations or exported to foreign countries for the benefit of foreign customers of these banks and corporations. So far as the people of the United States are concerned, the cupboard is bare."

"When the Federal Reserve Act was passed, the people of these United States did not perceive that a world banking system was being set up here. A super-state controlled by international bankers and industrialists...acting together to enslave the world...Every effort has been made by the Fed to conceal its powers but the truth is--the Fed has usurped the government."

JAMES MADISON

"The prime function of government is the protection of the different and unequal faculties of men for acquiring property."

"History records that the money changers have used every form of abuse, intrigue, deceit, and violent means possible to maintain their control over governments by controlling money and its issuance."

"The extension of the prohibition to bills of credit must give pleasure to every citizen, in proportion to his love of justice and his knowledge of the true springs of public prosperity. The loss which America has sustained since the peace from the pestilent effects of paper money on the necessary confidence between man and man, on the necessary confidence in the public councils, on the industry and morals of the people and on the character of republican government, constitutes an enormous debt against the States chargeable with this unadvised measure, which must long remain unsatisfied; or rather an accumulation of guilt, which can be expiated no otherwise than by a voluntary sacrifice on the altar of justice of the power which has been the instrument of it. In addition to these persuasive considerations, it may be observed that the same reasons which show the necessity of denying to the States the power of regulating coin, prove with equal force that they ought not to be at liberty to substitute a paper medium in the place of the coin." Number 44 of the Federalist Papers.

"Paper money may be deemed an aggression on the rights of the other states."

ALEXANDER HAMILTON

"To emit an unfunded paper as the sign of value ought not to continue a formal part of the Constitution, nor even hereafter to be employed; being, in its nature, pregnant with abuses, and liable to be made the engine of imposition and fraud; holding out temptations equally pernicious to the integrity of government and to the morals of the people."

ANDREW JACKSON

"If congress has the right under the Constitution to issue paper money, it was given them to use themselves, not to be delegated to individuals or corporations.

"The bold efforts that the present bank has made to control the government and the distress it has wantonly caused, are but premonitions of the fate which awaits the American people should they be deluded into a perpetuation of this institution or the establishment of another like it...If the people only understood the rank injustice of our money and banking system there would be a revolution before morning."

FROM A SECRET AGENT - 1862

"Slavery is likely to be abolished by the war power and all chattel slavery abolished. This I and my European friends are in favor of, for slavery is but the owning of labor and carries with it the care of the laborers, while the European plan, led on by England, is that capital shall control labor by controlling wages. The great debt that the capitalists will see to it is made out of the war, must be used as a means to control the volume of money. To accomplish this the bonds must be used as a banking basis. We are now waiting for the Secretary of the Treasury to make this recommendation to Congress. It will not do to allow the greenback, as it is called, to circulate as money any length of time, as we cannot control that. But we can control the bonds and through them the bank issues."

ABRAHAM LINCOLN

"There should be no war upon property or the owners of property. Property is the fruit of labor; property is desirable; is a positive good in the world. That some should be rich shows that others may become rich, hence, is just encouragement to industry and enterprise."

"I have two great enemies: the Southern Army in front of me, and the financial institutions to my rear. Of the two, the one in my rear is my greatest foe..."

"The Government should create, issue, and circulate all the currency and credits needed to satisfy the spending power of the Government and the buying power of consumers. By the adoption of these principles, the taxpayers will be saved immense sums of interest. Money will cease to be master and become the servant of humanity.

"Yes; we may all congratulate ourselves that this cruel war is nearing its close. It has cost a vast amount of treasure and blood. The best blood of the flower of American youth has been freely offered upon our country's altar that the Nation might live. It has been, indeed a trying hour for the Republic; but I see in the future a crisis approaching that unnerves me and causes me to tremble for the safety of my country. As a result of the war, corporations have been enthroned and an era of corruption in high places will follow, and the money power of the country will endeavor to prolong its reign by working upon the prejudices of the people until wealth is aggregated in a few hands and the Republic is destroyed. I feel at this moment more anxiety for the safety of my country than ever before, even in the midst of the war."

"I see in the near future a crisis approach which unnerves me and cause me to tremble for the safety of my country. Corporations (of banking) have been enthroned, an era of corruption in high places will follow, and the money power of the country will endeavor to prolong its reign by working upon the prejudices of the people until the wealth is aggregated in a few hands and the Republic destroyed."

SALMON P. CHASE, (Lincoln's Secretary to the Treasury) who was the pilot of the 1863 banking act in the US never forgave himself, subsequently saying:

"My agency, in promoting the passage of the National Bank Act, was the greatest mistake in my life. It has built up a monopoly which affects every interest in the country. It should be repealed, but before that can be accomplished, the people should be arrayed on one side, and the banks on the other, in a contest such as we have never seen before in this country."

OTTO VON BISMARCK, German Chancellor (1815-1898)

"The death of Lincoln was a disaster for Christendom. There was no man in the United States great enough to wear his boots and the bankers went anew to grab the riches. I fear that foreign bankers with their craftiness and tortuous tricks will entirely control the exuberant riches of America and use it to systematically corrupt modern civilization."

LONDON TIMES -1865

"If this mischievous financial policy [of creating a debt-free currency], which has its origin in the American Republic, shall become permanent, then that government will furnish its own money without cost! It will pay off its debts and be without debt. It will have all the money necessary to carry on its commerce. It will become prosperous without precedent in the history of the world. The brains and the wealth of all countries will go to America. That government must be destroyed or it will destroy every monarchy on the globe!"

JOHN C. CALHOUN

"A power has risen up in the government greater than the people themselves, consisting of many and various powerful interests combined in one mass, and held together by the cohesive power of the vast surplus in the banks."

LEON N. TOLSTOY

"Money is a new form of slavery, and distinguishable from the old simply by the fact that it is impersonal -- that there is no human relation between master and slave."

FREDERIC BASTIAT, THE LAW

"When plunder becomes a way of life for a group of men living together in society, they create for themselves in the course of time a legal system that authorizes it and a moral code that glorifies it."

WN. COBBETT

"I set to work to read the Act of Parliament by which the Bank of England was created in 1694. The inventors knew well what they were about. Their design was to mortgage by degrees the whole of the country, all the lands, all the houses, and all other property, and even all labor, to those who would lend their money to the State—the scheme, the crafty, the cunning, the deep scheme has produced what the world never saw before—starvation in the midst of plenty."

DARRYL R. FRANCIS, former President of the Federal Reserve Bank of St. Louis

"Since the direct method of printing money to finance government expenditures is prohibited in the United states, the monetization of government deficits has occurred indirectly . . . government debt is ultimately being financed by the creation of new money . . . I doubt that monetization of debt has a conscious act . . . I can find no benefits accruing to the whole of society from debt monetization, but the risks are very serious and can be expressed in one word, inflation" "In the case of debt monetization the immediate and even the short run impact is neither an increase in interest rates, and yet real resources are still being transferred from **private to government use."**

Page 24 "Federal Reserve System" Bd. of Gov.'s

"....in the practical workings of the banking system the bulk of deposits originates in the granting of loans....and his ability to make loans and investments arise largely from the receipt of his depositors' money."

"As we realize that banks create their own deposit debts....we begin to see why these institutions are often referred to as monetizers of debt..."

Federal Reserve Bank of Chicago, Modern Money Mechanics

"The actual process of money creation takes place in commercial banks. As noted earlier, demand liabilities of commercial banks are money.", p.3.

"Confidence in these forms of money also seems to be tied in some way to the fact that assets exist on the books of the government and the banks equal to the amount of money outstanding, even though most of the assets themselves are no more than pieces of paper--.", P.3.

"Commercial banks create checkbook money whenever they grant a loan, simply by adding new deposit dollars in accounts on their books in exchange for a borrower's IOU.", p. 19.

"The 12 regional reserve banks aren't government institutions, but corporations nominally 'owned' by member commercial banks.", p. 27.

St. Louis Federal Reserve Bank, Review, Nov. 1975, p.22

"The decrease in purchasing power incurred by holders of money due to inflation imparts gains to the issuers of money--."

Federal Reserve Bank of Philadelphia, Gold, p. 10

"Without the confidence factor, many believe a paper money system is liable to collapse eventually."

Federal Reserve Bank, New York

"Because of 'fractional' reserve system, banks, as a whole, can expand our money supply several times, by making loans and investments."

"Commercial banks create checkbook money whenever they grant a loan, simply by adding new deposit dollars in accounts on their books in exchange for a borrower's IOU."

Federal Reserve Bank of Chicago

"The actual process of money creation takes place in commercial banks. As noted earlier, demand liabilities of commercial banks are money."

ROBERT HEMPHILL, former Credit Manager of the Federal Reserve Bank in Atlanta.

"If all the bank loans were paid, no one could have a bank deposit, and there would not be a dollar of coin or currency in circulation. This is a staggering thought. We are completely dependent on the commercial banks. Someone has to borrow every dollar we have in circulation, cash, or credit. If the banks create ample synthetic money we are prosperous; if not, we starve. We are absolutely without a permanent money system. When one gets a complete grasp of the picture, the tragic absurdity of our hopeless situation is almost incredible-but there it is."

WALTER WRISTON
Former chairman of the Citicorp Bank

"If we had a truth-in-Government act comparable to the truth-in-advertising law, every note issued by the Treasury would be obliged to include a sentence stating: "This note will be redeemed with the proceeds from an identical note which will be sold to the public when this one comes due." When this activity is carried out in the United States, as it is weekly, it is described as a Treasury bill auction. But when basically the same process is conducted abroad in a foreign language, our news media usually speak of a country's "rolling over its debts." The perception remains that some form of disaster is inevitable. It is not. To see why, it is only necessary to understand the basic facts of government borrowing. The first is that there are few recorded instances in history of government - any government - actually getting out of debt. Certainly in an era of $100-billion deficits, no one lending money to our Government by buying a Treasury bill expects that it will be paid at maturity in any way except by our Government's selling a new bill of like amount."

MERRILL JENKINS SR.

"The right of distribution over private property is the essence of freedom." "Force- modern Money, then, has the power to create debt since it can command other goods, but is valueless itself. Money has purchasing power, but no value -- without purchasing power.. Fed. "Notes" must be accepted as a tender for debt, but are not "money" -- so therefore -- do not have money's unique ability called purchasing power, what thing has purchasing power? What thing can force the public to offer its property and rights? Offer means to present for action or consideration; propose; suggest; it is a voluntary act. What thing can 'force' anyone into a voluntary act of offering? The words force and voluntary are exactly opposed and it is by the acceptance of this impossible concept of 'voluntary force' being 'purchasing power' that makes the public believe that something must be 'money' and have this unique power."

CONGRESSMAN JERRY VOORHIS

"The banks -- commercial banks and the Federal Reserve -- create all the money of this nation and its people pay interest on every dollar of that newly created money. Which means that private banks exercise unconstitutionally, immorally, and ridiculously the power to tax the people. For every newly created dollar dilutes to some extent the value of every other dollar already in circulation."

RUSSELL L.MUNK

Former Assistant General Counsel, Department of the Treasury

"Federal Reserve Notes are not dollars."

PRESIDENT JOHN ADAMS

"All the perplexities, confusions and distresses in America arise not from defects in the constitution or confederation, not from want of honor or virtue, as much as from downright ignorance of the nature of coin, credit and circulation."

THE CONSTITUTION OF THE UNITED STATES OF AMERICA

"No State shall enter into any treaty, alliance, or confederation; grant letters of marque and reprisal; coin money; emit letters of credit; make anything but gold and silver coin a tender in payment of debts; pass any bill of attainder, ex post facto law, or law impairing the obligation of contracts, or grant any title of nobility." (Article I, Section 10)

U.S. Supreme Court, Craig v. Missouri, 4 Peters 410.

"Emitting bills of credit, or the creation of money by private corporations, is what is expressly forbidden by Article 1, Section 10 of the U.S. Constitution."

GEORGE BANCROFT

"Madison, agreeing with the journal of the convention, records that the grant of power to emit bills of credit was refused by a majority of more than four to one. The evidence is perfect; no power to emit paper money was granted to the legislature of the United States."

JOHN FISKE

"It was finally decided, by the vote of nine states against New Jersey and Maryland, that the power to issue inconvertible paper should not be granted to the federal government. An express prohibition, such as had been adopted for the separate states, was thought unnecessary. It was supposed that it was enough to withhold the power, since the federal government would not venture to exercise it unless expressly permitted in the Constitution. "Thus," says Madison, in his narrative of the proceedings, "the pretext for a paper currency, and particularly for making the bills a tender, either for public or private debts, was cut off." Nothing could be more clearly expressed than this. As Mr. Justice Field observes, in his able dissenting opinion in the recent case of Juilliard vs. Greenman, "if there be anything in the history of the Constitution which can be established with moral certainty, it is that the framers of that instrument intended to prohibit the issue of legal-tender notes both by the general government and by the states, and thus prevent interference with the contracts of private parties." Such has been the opinion of our ablest constitutional jurists, Marshall, Webster, Story, Curtis, and Nelson. There can be little doubt that, according to all sound principles of interpretation, the Legal Tender Act of 1862 was passed in flagrant violation of the Constitution."

CONGRESSIONAL RECORD, MAY 11, 1972

"Some people think the Federal Reserve Banks are United States government institutions, they are not government institutions, they are private credit monopolies."

"The Federal Reserve Board and the Federal Reserve Banks are private Corporations."

JOHN MAYNARD KEYNES
(Chief architect of our current fiat-paper money system)

"By a continuing process of inflation, governments can confiscate, secretly and unobserved, an important part of the wealth of their citizens"

"If governments should refrain from regulation..... the worthlessness of the money becomes apparent and the fraud upon the public can be concealed no longer"

"Lenin is said to have declared that the best way to destroy the Capitalistic System was to debauch the currency. . . Lenin was certainly right. There is no subtler, no surer means of overturning the existing basis of society than to debauch the currency. The process engages all the hidden forces of economic law on the side of destruction, and does it in a manner which not one man in a million can diagnose."

CHARLES LINDBERG

"Ever since the Civil War, Congress has allowed the bankers to control financial legislation. The membership of the Finance Committee in the Senate (now the Banking and Currency Committee) and the Committee on Banking and Currency in the House have been made up chiefly of bankers, their agents, and their attorneys. ...In this way the committees have been able to control legislation in the interests of the few."

"This Act (Federal Reserve Act) establishes the most gigantic trust on earth. When the President signs this bill, the invisible government by the Monetary Power will be legalized... The worst legislative crime of the age is perpetrated by this banking and currency bill. The caucus of the party bosses have again operated and prevented the people from getting the benefits of their own government."

BENJAMIN DISRAELI, former British Prime Minister

"The world is Governed by very different personages from what is imagined by those who are not behind the scenes."

WILLIAM JENNINGS BRYAN

"Money power denounces, as public enemies, all who question its methods or throw light upon its crimes."

JOHN F. KENNEDY

"The great free nations of the world must take control of our monetary problems if these problems are not to take control of us."

ERNEST HEMINGWAY

"The first panacea for a mismanaged nation is inflation of the currency; second is war. Both bring a temporary (and false) prosperity; both bring a permanent ruin. But both are the refuge of political and economic opportunities."

THE RT. HON. REGINALD MCKENNA

(one-time British Chancellor of the Exchequer, and Chairman of the Midland Bank)
"I am afraid the ordinary citizen will not like to be told that the banks can, and do, create and destroy money. The amount of finance in existence varies only with the action of the banks in increasing or decreasing deposits and bank purchases. We know how this is affected. Every loan, overdraft or bank purchase creates a deposit, and every repayment of a loan, overdraft or bank sale destroys a deposit."

"And they who control the credit of the nation direct the policy of governments, and hold in the hollow of their hands the destiny of the people."

JOHN B. RARICK

"Mr. Speaker, the current efforts by our Government to hold down price increases have served to focus the attention of thoughtful students on a little discussed facet of our money system, this system, because of a long procedure of miseducation and studied silence, is not now understood as it was prior to the adoption of the Federal Reserve system more than half a century ago. It is based upon debt; has serious implications for the future of our country, and invites what may be the greatest war in history. ... Every debt Dollar demands an interest tribute from our economy for every year that Dollar remains in circulation. These interest costs force up the price of every commodity and service and contribute greatly to inflation. ..."

"Under the Constitution, the Congress has responsibility of issuing the nation's money and regulating its value Art. 1, Sec 8, Cl. 5, in a recent brilliant analysis of our money system by T. David Horton, Chairman of the Executive Council of the Defenders of the American Constitution, able Lawyer and keen student of basic American history, he suggests a proven remedy for our current predicament that will enable the Congress to resume its Constitutional responsibilities to regulate our nation's money by liberating our economy from the swindle of the debt-money manipulators by the issuance of national currency in debt free form ... We have a certain amount of non-interest bearing money in circulation, all of our fractional currency, pennies, nickels, dimes, quarters, and half dollars. They are manufactured in our mints, and are paid into circulation, circulate freely, and provide the government with a valuable source of revenue. From 1966 through 1970 the amount of seignorage paid into the treasury by the mints amounted to in excess of 4 billion dollars the profit ratio on this type of currency is 6 to 1, or currency 6 times the cost of production. The cost ration for Federal Reserve Notes is 600 to 1; however, during these same four years, 1966 through 1970, 50 billion dollars in Federal Reserve Notes were manufactured by the bureau of printing and engraving and turned over to the banks; not one cent in seignorage was paid over to the treasury. ... Our Debt money system compels the government to spend more than it takes in, because this is the only way we can keep the economy going..."

GEORGE WASHINGTON

"Every lover of his country will therefore be solicitous to find out some speedy remedy for this alarming evil. There is no possible substitute for the loss of commerce. Our first grand object, therefore, is its restoration. I presume not to dictate or direct. It is a subject that will require the deepest deliberations and researches of the wisest and more experienced men in America to fully comprehend. It probably belongs to no one man existing to possess all the qualifications required to trace the course of American commerce through all intricate paths and to those and only those that shall lead the United States to future glory and prosperity I am sanguine in the belief of the possibility that we may one day become a great commercial and flourishing nation. But if in the pursuit of the means we should unfortunately stumble again on unfunded paper money or any similar species of fraud, we shall assuredly give a fatal stab to our national credit in its infancy. Paper money will invariably operate in the body of politics as spirit liquors on the human body. They prey on the vitals and ultimately destroy them."
"Paper money has had the effect in your state that it will ever have, to ruin commerce, oppress the honest, and open the door to every species of fraud and injustice." (Letter to J. Bowen, Rhode Island, Jan. 9, 1787)

"If ever again our nation stumbles upon unfunded paper, it shall surely be like death to our body politic. This country will crash."

JERRY JORDAN, Cleveland Fed Res Bank President

"The failed attempts at influencing real economic activity during the late 1960's and 1970's are a clear warning of the damaging power of the central bank."

DENNIS KARNOFSKY, Chief economic adviser St. Louis Federal Reserve Bank

"....what is a dollar it's just something artificial we throw out there....what you're doing is you're fooling people...."

LAWRENCE PARKS, Executive Director, FAME

"Bypassing voters, taxpayers and the public at large, Congress has delegated to the Fed a power that the Congress itself does not have."

LUDWIG VON MISES

"Government is the only agency which can take a useful commodity like paper, slap some ink on it and make it totally worthless."

DANIEL WEBSTER

"No other rights are safe where property is not safe:"

"Of all the contrivances devised for cheating the laboring classes of mankind, none has been more effective than that which deludes him with paper money."

"We are in danger of being overwhelmed with irredeemable paper, mere paper, representing not gold nor silver; no sir, representing nothing but broken promises, bad faith, bankrupt corporations, cheated creditors and a ruined people."

PELATIAH WEBSTER

"Paper money polluted the equity of our laws, turned them into engines of oppression, corrupted the justice of our public

44

administration, destroyed the fortunes of thousands who had confidence in it, enervated the trade, husbandry, and manufactures of our country, and went far to destroy the morality of our people."

BENJAMIN FRANKLIN

"The refusal of King George to operate an honest colonial money system which freed the ordinary man from the clutches of the manipulators was probably the prime cause of the Revolution."
"The Colonies would gladly have borne the little tax on tea and other matters, had it not been that England took away from the Colonies their money, which created unemployment and dissatisfaction."

THOMAS JEFFERSON

"The system of banking we have both equally and ever reprobated. I contemplate it as a blot left in all our constitutions, which, if not covered, will end in their destruction, ... I sincerely believe, with you, that banking establishments are more dangerous than standing armies; and that the principle of spending money to be paid by posterity, under the name of funding, is but swindling futurity on a large scale."

"The eyes of our citizens are not sufficiently open to the true cause of our distress. They ascribe them to everything but their true cause, the banking system; a system which if it could do good in any form is yet so certain of leading to abuse as to be utterly incompatible with the public safety and prosperity. I sincerely believe that banking establishments are more dangerous than standing armies... and that the principle of spending money to be paid by posterity, under the name of funding, is but swindling futurity on a large scale."

"... we must not let our rulers load us with perpetual debt...If we run into such debts as that we must be taxed in our meat and in our drink, in our necessities and comforts, in our labors and in our amusements, for our callings and our creeds...our people...must come to labor 16 hours in the 24, give the earnings of 15 of these to the government for their debts and daily expenses; and the 16th being insufficient to afford us bread,...We have no time to think, no means of calling the mis-managers to account; but be glad to obtain subsistence by hiring ourselves, to rivet their chains on the necks of our fellow sufferers. Our land holders, too...retaining indeed the title and stewardship of estates called theirs, but held really in trust for the treasury,. . .this is the tendency of all human governments. A departure from principle becomes a precedent for a second; that second for a third; and so on, till the bulk of society is reduced to mere automatons of misery, to have no sensibilities left but for sinning and suffering...And the fore horse of this frightful team is public debt. Taxation follows that, and in its train, wretchedness and oppression."

"I believe that banking institutions are more dangerous to our liberties than standing armies. Already they have raised up a money aristocracy that has set the government at defiance. This issuing power should be taken from the banks and restored to the people to whom it properly belongs. If the American people ever allow private banks to control the issue of currency, first by inflation, then by deflation, the banks and corporations that will grow up around them will deprive the people of all property until their children will wake up homeless on the continent their fathers conquered. I hope we shall crush in its birth the aristocracy of the moneyed corporations which already dare to challenge our Government to a trial of strength and bid defiance to the laws of our country"

"I place economy among the first and important virtues, and public debt as the greatest of dangers. To preserve our independence, we must not let our rulers load us with perpetual debt. We must make our choice between economy and liberty, or profusion and servitude. If we can prevent the government from wasting the labors of the people under the pretense of caring for them, they will be happy."

"The Central Bank is an institution of the most deadly hostility existing against the principles and form of our Constitution."

GEORGE BANCROFT

"Madison, agreeing with the journal of the convention, records that the grant of power to emit bills of credit was refused by a majority of more than four to one. The evidence is perfect; no power to emit paper money was granted to the legislature of the United States."

THOMAS A. EDISON

"People who will not turn a shovel of dirt on the project, nor contribute a pound of material, will collect more money, from the United States, than will the people, who supply all the material and do all the work. This is the terrible thing about interest (usury) ... But here is the point: If the nation can issue a dollar bond, it can also issue a dollar bill. The element that makes the bond good, makes the bill good, also. The difference, between the bond and the bill, is that the bond lets the money-broker collect twice the amount of the bond, and an additional 20%. Whereas the currency, the honest sort, provided by the Constitution, pays nobody, but those, who contribute in some useful way. It is absurd, to say that our country can issue bonds, and cannot issue currency. Both are promises to pay, but one fattens the usurer and the other helps the people. If the currency issued by the people were no good, then the bonds would be no good, either. It is a terrible situation, when the Government, to insure the national wealth, must go in debt and submit to ruinous interest charges, at the hands of men, who control the fictitious value of gold. Interest is the invention of Satan."

Mr. Phillip A. Benson, President of the American Bankers' Association, June 8 1939

"There is no more direct way to capture control of a nation than through its credit (money) system."

F.A. HAYEK

"The history of government management of money has, except for a few short happy periods, been one of incessant fraud and deception."

DR. PAUL HEIN

"Freedom and fiat are incompatible; slavery and scrip are bedfellows."

"Inflation (caused by paper money) is an evil which exerts its baleful influence throughout society. Gold and silver were gifts of God, and, short of the labor required to obtain them, were ours free. They didn't have to be returned to the source, much less with interest! Inflation, on the other hand, is borrowed into existence from a privileged clique who, by the very nature of the process, enslave those who use it."

USA Banker's Magazine, August 25 1924

"Capital must protect itself in every possible manner by combination and legislation. Debts must be collected, bonds and mortgages must be foreclosed as rapidly as possible. When, through a process of law, the common people lose their homes they will become more docile and more easily governed through the influence of the strong arm of government, applied by a central power of wealth under control of leading financiers. This truth is well known among our principal men now engaged in forming an imperialism of Capital to govern the world. By dividing the voters through the political party system, we can get them to expend their energies in fighting over questions of no importance. Thus by discreet action we can secure for ourselves what has been so well planned and so successfully accomplished."

Treasury Secretary Woodin, 3/7/1933

"Where would we be if we had I.O.U.'s scrip and certificates floating all around the country?" Instead he decided to "issue currency against the sound assets of the banks. The Federal Reserve Act lets us print all we'll need. And it won't frighten the people. It won't look like stage money. It'll be money that looks like real money." The Bank Holiday of 1933', p20

President Franklin D. Roosevelt

"The real truth of the matter is, as you and I know, that a financial element in the large centers has owned the government ever since the days of Andrew Jackson."

John Kenneth Galbraith

"The study of money, above all other fields in economics, is one in which complexity is used to disguise truth or to evade truth, not to reveal it." Money: Whence it came, where it went - 1975, p15
"The process by which banks create money is so simple that the mind is repelled." Money: Whence it came, where it went - 1975, p29

DR. CARROLL QUIGLEY
Georgetown professor (Bill Clinton's mentor)

"... nothing less than to create a world system of financial control in private hands able to dominate the political system of each country and the economy of the worlds a whole... controlled in a feudalist fashion by the central banks of the world acting in concert, by secret agreements arrived at in frequent private meetings and conferences."

BOB PRECHTER

"I cannot morally blame all Americans for allowing, for instance, the birth of the Federal Reserve System (a private cartel with full control over the issuance of national debt) and the money destruction that has followed. They are simply ignorant about it and don't know what happened or what is happening. They think that prices go up rather than that dollars go down. Unsound money imposes an environment of immorality, which in turn makes people behave in different ways for reasons they know not. Sometimes you can blame immorality for the imposition of bad structures (bad people do it with full knowledge of what they are doing), but sometimes it is simply stupidity. People revere democracy, but democracy ends in plunder by the majority. Are people immoral for supporting democracy? I think rather that they lack a deep understanding of its essence. At a very deep level, I would say that the reason such structures are created is due to both a lack of knowledge and a false morality, which in turn is due to a lack of knowledge."

REP. HOWARD BUFFETT

"The gold standard acted as a silent watchdog to prevent 'unlimited public spending.' Our finances will never be brought in order until Congress is compelled to do so. Making our money redeemable in gold will create this compulsion."

". . . when you recall that one of the first moves by Lenin, Mussolini and Hitler was to outlaw individual ownership of gold, you begin to sense that there may be some connection between money, redeemable in gold, and the rare prize known as human liberty. Also, when you find that Lenin declared and demonstrated that a sure way to overturn the existing social order and bring about communism was by printing press paper money, then again you are impressed with the possibility of a relationship between a gold-backed money and human freedom."

Encyclopedia Britannica, 14th Edition

"Banks create credit. It is a mistake to suppose that bank credit is created to any extent by the payment of money into the banks. A loan made by a bank is a clear addition to the amount of money in the community."

50

"The abandonment of the gold standard made it possible for the welfare statists to use the banking system as a means to an unlimited expansion of credit.... **In the absence of the gold standard, there is no way to protect savings from confiscation through inflation.*** There is no safe store of value.... Deficit spending is simply a scheme for the "hidden" confiscation of wealth.... [Gold] stands as a protector of property rights."

"This is the shabby secret of the welfare statists' tirades against gold. Deficit spending is simply a scheme for the "hidden" confiscation of wealth. Gold stands in the way of this insidious process. It stands as a protector of property rights. If one grasps this, one has no difficulty in understanding the statists' antagonism toward the gold standard."

Alan Greenspan's statement is only partly true. A method could be devised, by creating a board consisting of congressmen and state's governors, that would assure that paper money without gold and silver backing, would not be produced that exceeded the country's GDP.

-Part Two-
Additions to Billions for the Bankers...
By Larry Flinchpaugh
©

After reading Sheldon Emery's original 1984 publication and my comments in the "Introduction" and "Conclusion" of this booklet, it is my hope that you will understand the importance of abolishing the *privately owned* Federal Reserve Banking System and Fractional Reserve Banking and will write your congressmen and advise all with whom you come in contact, the importance of this issue. Not only should the *privately owned* Federal Reserve System be abolished, but in my opinion *all the money that our government (the tax payer) currently owes to the Fed should be written off.*

In 2012 the national debt is over 15 trillion dollars with some claiming that 45% of that debt is owed to the private Federal Reserve banking cartel. (*Kansas City Fed Pres. claims it is about 24%)*

In other words the United States government would be justified in claiming "Bankruptcy" and starting over *without* the Federal Reserve. This write off of 6.75 trillion dollars (.45 x 15 trillion) would be only a small fraction of the trillions of dollars the Federal Reserve has stolen from the American people since 1913. Congressman Ron Paul has introduced a bill advocating writing off $1.6 trillion owed to the Federal Reserve.

As you study this issue, you will gradually begin to understand why the **Private** *Federal Reserve* System and *Fractional Reserve Banking* must be abolished, why we must once again abide by the Constitution, and why we need to stop being the "policeman" of the world. **Henry Ford** was quoted as saying, "It is well enough that the people of this nation do not understand our banking and monetary system, for if they did, I believe there would be a revolution before tomorrow morning."

Most likely your current news sources and formal education has misinformed you with outright lies, lack of information, false fears and propaganda that has completely distorted your views of our monetary system.

As you study our current monetary system, you will find that if the Federal Reserve banking system were abolished, there would be no need to collect income taxes on people's wages. *The taxes collected on your wages do not go to pay for services but rather to pay for the interest the* **Private** *Federal Reserve charges the tax payers for printing and loaning us our own money.* Just think what an improvement, not only in your life, but also the improvement in your entire community, if you were **not** required to pay income tax on your wages.

The elite bankers, the crooked politicians, and the controlled mainstream media will attempt to silence those of us calling for the abolishment of unconstitutional income tax on our wages by calling us "Un-American" for rebelling against paying *"our fair share"* of income taxes. We are not rebelling against paying income taxes—only income tax on our wages. Do not be fooled or intimidated by their tactics. You are more of a patriotic American than they by abiding by the Constitution and by advocating returning control of our monetary system back to the people. The IRS would still be needed to collect the legitimate taxes on business profits, gains on stocks and bonds, and profits from selling **commercial** real estate.

Imagine buying a house, a car, or obtaining a small loan to start a business and not being required to pay interest, (usury as prohibited in the Bible). Don't let anyone tell you that this is a stupid idea or that it would simply not work. It will work! In some Middle Eastern Muslim countries it is working. Critics might argue that the fees charged by the banks in these Muslim countries are close to what others call interest. However, it is not even close.

It is not a coincidence that most of our country's so called enemies are those who are *not* controlled by the international bankers. You can rest assured when the U.S. is successful in over throwing Libya, their government controlled bank will end up with a central Bank controlled by the international bankers.

The government, the mass media, our educational system, and religious organizations have lied to us about how our government really works and who actually controls us behind the scenes. Some have referred to the bankers who control us as "*The Men Behind the Curtain*" or the *"Shadow Government."* Every time we go through a business cycle of boom and bust, the elite banksters make billions of dollars at the expense of the common citizen. Remember that when we experience a recession or depression "wealth is not lost." It is merely transferred from the poor and middle class to the wealthy.

The next time you vote for a Democrat or Republican candidate in a presidential election and believe that you are instrumental in **electing** the president, just remember, someone else **selected** the president you will be voting for. It doesn't even matter which party wins. Both are controlled by the same puppet masters.

The patriarch of the Rothschild banking dynasty, Mayer Amschel Rothschild (1744-1812) once said, "Give me control of a nation's money and I care not who makes its laws."

There is about as much difference between the Democrats and Republicans today as there is between Coke and Pepsi.

History of Money and Banking

Contrary to popular belief our monetary system does not need and never has needed to be backed by gold or silver. (Except to be constitutional) Granted, precious metal backing could limit the amount of paper money put into circulation and help keep inflation under control, but the same thing can be accomplished by tying the amount of money to be printed to the yearly increase in our country's Gross Domestic Product. (GDP) In this way the money is backed by sweat (value added) and an increase in production. This "value added" plus our government's acceptance of this paper money for the payment of taxes is all that is need for backing.

The first bankers were the **goldsmiths** who accepted bullion and coins for safe keeping and would give the owner a receipt for his deposit. The owner soon discovered that it was easier to use his receipt to pay for goods and services than to use the actual gold. Since the receipt holders rarely demanded their gold all at the same time, the ***goldsmiths realized they could profit enormously by making more loans than they had gold on hand.*** Gradually the goldsmiths became bankers as they stopped manufacturing gold items and replaced it with lending activities. In this way banks began to create money. This was the beginning of our modern banking system.

Let's review the history of money and banking as it has evolved in the Unites States.

Barter

For commerce to work efficiently there must be a medium of exchange. In the distant past "Barter" was the only method of exchange because money with intrinsic value, gold, silver and copper coins, didn't exist. Barter worked fairly smoothly as long as both parties needed the products or services of the other. When this wasn't the case the trade couldn't be made and was complicated by requiring additional time and travel to find someone to trade with.

Before the American colonists had signed the U.S. Constitution their money consisted mainly in the trading of beaver pelts, tobacco, farm products, handmade items, etc. and colorful wampum shells and beads that were in high demand among the Indian tribes.

Metal Coins

The Romans and Greeks solved the problems involved in bartering by using rare metals to produce gold, silver and copper coins with intrinsic value because of their scarcity. Also these rare metals could be used to produce beautiful jewelry and works of art and cooking utensils.

As time passed the colonist used almost any foreign coins but the Spanish silver dollar was preferred. The Spanish dollar was divided into what was called bits. A bit was valued at 12 ½ cents, two bits equaled a quarter, four bits a half dollar and eight bits was equal to a full dollar. Even as late as the 1940's people in the rural areas of our country priced things in "Bits." As a youngster, visiting my cousin Mike in Breckenridge, Missouri, I was confronted with this oddity and had to learn what a "bit" would buy at the local Variety Store or Grocery Store.

After signing the Constitution, states began to produce their own state coins and "Bank Notes" **Article 1 Section 8** gives the U.S. Congress the power "To coin Money, regulate the Value thereof, and of foreign Coin, and fix the Standard of Weights and Measures;.." It should be noted here that "coin money" meant metal coins like gold, silver, and copper. Paper money was not considered as money at all but rather a debt instrument promising to pay the bearer on demand in gold or silver.

Keep in mind that when you use gold or silver coins as money or paper money (notes) backed by gold or silver, you are still engaged in bartering. Instead of trading a fish for a basket, you are trading gold or silver for a basket.

<u>Silver Certificates</u> are a type of representative money printed from 1878 to 1964 in the United States. (Redeemable in silver)

<u>Gold certificates</u> in general are certificates of ownership that gold owners hold instead of storing the actual gold (Redeemable in gold). They were used as US paper currency (1882–1933). When the U.S. was taken off the gold standard in 1933, gold certificates were withdrawn from circulation.

Economics Lesson 2011

• **U.S. Tax revenue: $2,170,000,000,000**
• **Fed budget: $3,820,000,000,000**
• **New debt: $ 1,650,000,000,000**
• **National debt: $14,271,000,000,000**
• **Recent budget cut: $ 38,500,000,000**
Now, remove 8 zeros and pretend it's a household budget.

- **Annual family income: $21,700**
- **Money the family spent: $38,200**
- **New debt on the credit card: $16,500**
- **Outstanding balance on credit card: $142,710**
- **Total budget cuts: $385**

Sorta brings the issue "home" doesn't it?

Note: There are two ways to collect funds to run the Federal Government;   (1) The transparent and honest way is to collect taxes and (2) the deceptive and dishonest way   is debt financing (borrowing with interest) taking advantage of the hidden inflation tax because of the increase in the money supply.   (Prices keep going up and the people falsely blame the farmer, grocery stores, the oil companies, etc. when in reality prices are going up because the purchasing value of the dollar is going down.)

Following is an example how an increase in the money supply causes prices to increase.   Suppose you and 10 other people are at an auction bidding on a particular item.   The auctioneer pauses for a moment and gives each bidder a gift of $100.00 (increase in the money supply) immediately each bidder starts bidding more because of the increase in his money supply.

Executive Order 6102
April 5, 1933
By
President Franklin D. Roosevelt

The bank panics of February/March 1933 and foreign exchange movements were in danger of exhausting the Federal Reserve holdings of gold.   Executive order 6102 forbids the Hoarding of Gold   Coin,   Gold Bullion,   and Gold   Certificates   by   U.S. citizens.

The order criminalized the American public's ability to own gold as an investment vehicle. It required U.S. citizens to deliver all but a small amount of gold coin, gold bullion, and gold certificates owned by them to the Federal Reserve, in exchange for $20.67 per troy ounce. Under the "Trading With the Enemies Act" of October 6, 1917, as amended on March 9, 1933, violation of the order was punishable by a fine up to $10,000 ($167,700 if adjusted for inflation as of 2010) or up to ten years in prison, or both. Most citizens who owned large amounts of gold had it transferred to countries such as Switzerland.

The price of gold from the Treasury for international transactions was thereafter raised to $35 an ounce ($587 in 2010 dollars). The resulting profit that the government realized funded the Exchange Stabilization Fund established by the Gold Reserve Act in 1934.

President Nixon Ends the gold standard for US dollars in 1971

This action cancelled the direct convertibility of the United States dollar to gold. The Federal Reserve is not obliged to tie the dollar to anything. No longer would you see a "Silver Certificate" stating that it could be traded for real money (silver) at your local bank. Today you could trade a "Federal Reserve" one dollar bill for a so called silver dollar but today's silver dollars found at the banks do not consist of 1 ounce of silver.

Banking Systems:

Timeline of central banking in the United States

- 1781   Bank of North America
- 1791–1811:   First Bank of the United States
- 1811–1816:   No central bank
- 1816–1836:   Second Bank of the United States

- 1837–1862:   Free Bank Era
- 1846–1921:   Independent Treasury System
- 1863–1913:   National Banks
- 1913–Present: Federal Reserve System

Bank of North America (1781 in Philadelphia) was established by an act of the Congress of the Confederation where it followed the state-chartered Bank of Pennsylvania founded in 1780. It helped to fund the American Revolutionary War.

Robert Morris, the first Superintendent of Finance, saw a national, for-profit, private monopoly as an extension of the Bank of England as necessary, because previous attempts to finance the Revolutionary War with continental currency emitted by the Continental Congress, had led to depreciation to such an extent that Alexander Hamilton considered them to be "public embarrassments."

After the war, a number of state banks were chartered, including in 1784: the Bank of New York and the Bank of Massachusetts.

First Bank of the United States Congress chartered in 1791 to succeed the Bank of North America under Article One, Section 8. However, Congress failed to renew the charter for the Bank of the United States, which expired in 1811.

Second Bank of the United States was chartered in 1816 and then closed in 1836.

Federal Reserve Act of 1913 again established and permitted a private bank for profit to print, control and loan money to our government and charge the tax payer interest for this service. This brought all banks in the United States under the authority of the Federal Reserve (a quasi-governmental entity), creating the twelve regional Federal Reserve Banks.

After the passage of the Federal Reserve Act in 1913, in order to finance the government when tax revenues and other sources were not available, the United States Congress had to borrow money with interest from a private banking cartel- "The Federal Reserve." Before 1913 Congress could print its own **interest free** treasury notes instead of **interest bearing** Federal Reserve notes. This was a huge change in government finance much to the detriment of society.

The deceptive Federal Reserve Act was in the best interest of a few bankers but was a disaster for the American citizen. Since the Federal Reserve was established, the private bankers have looted us citizens out of trillions of dollars. (The dollar has lost over 90% of its purchasing value.)

Federal Reserve Building Washington D.C.

The Federal Reserve is a privately owned Bank established by the 1913 Federal Reserve Act. This Act authorizes them to print our country's money supply (Federal Reserve Notes) and charge the American taxpayer interest for loaning us our own money. This *scam* is absolutely not necessary. The Treasury Department can simply issue our currency **interest free**.

-Part Three-
Credit as a Public Utility
By: Larry Flinchpaugh

The profound concept of "Credit as a Public Utility" is going to sound rather strange to most people reading this booklet. Whether this concept can ever be adopted is questionable, but understanding the principal involved is basic to coming up with viable solutions to our monetary problems.

As stated earlier, the private Federal Reserve that charges the taxpayer interest for creating and printing their own money must be abolished and the U.S. Treasury Department must be allowed to print *Interest free U.S. Treasury notes* instead of *Interest bearing Federal Reserve notes.*

To review, the advantages to this would be:

(1) The citizens of this country would not have to pay income tax on their salaries. This would give a 20-25% raise in income for many citizens and even more for those in the higher income brackets. President Reagan commissioned a study which found the federal revenue collected from taxing citizens' wages was used to mainly pay for the interest that the Federal Reserve charged and was not used to pay for government services.

(2) The chance of having continuous unnecessary wars and conflicts would be greatly diminished. If *debt financing* through the Federal Reserve, which creates money out of thin air and causes inflation to soar, was no longer available, the money would have to come from transparent taxes. Can you imagine what the reaction would be by the tax payer if President Obama appeared on the evening news and said, "My fellow Americans, I have decided to nuke Iran tomorrow and we just don't have the money to pay for it. Therefore I am announcing that immediately everyone will see a 40-50% increase in their income taxes." What do you think the results would be? I doubt very much we would go to war under this scenario.

Out of the *fifteen trillion* dollars of U.S. debt, it is estimated that between 1.7 and 6.7 *trillion* dollars is "owed" to the private

Federal Reserve Bank. Since our country is bankrupt and the use of the Federal Reserve is unconstitutional, we should simply abolish the Fed and write off the amount the taxpayers' "owe" them. This would be quite a stimulus to our economy and at the same time be retribution for all the money the Fed has stolen from the American people since 1913. *The Kansas City Fed President claims that the taxpayers owe the Fed. about 24% or $3.6 Trillion. Others claim it is as much as 45% or $6.7 trillion.*

At the state level, only banks owned by the state should be allowed to engage in *Fractional Reserve Banking.* The profit from loaning other people's money would then go to the taxpayers who owned the bank instead to the private banking corporations like Wells Fargo, US Bank, Chase, etc. These private banks could still be your local bank but could only *loan their own money.* Most public works projects could then be financed *interest free* through state owned banks because of the profit generated using Fractional Reserve Banking. Again, the bank profit would be the taxpayer's profit instead of a private bank's profit.

Under our current system when the GDP (Gross Domestic Product) exceeds the amount of money or credit available, this "Gap" between production and consumption can only be filled by the consumer borrowing from the banks with interest.

Why not allow the consumer to benefit from this imbalance between production and consumption instead of a private bank? In order to do this, the Federal government could give each American adult a *dividend* check. The creation of this *dividend* would not be inflationary because there was already production to back it up. A few years ago this gap amounted to ten thousand dollars for each American adult.

The monetary system that we have now mainly benefits the Banksters because credit is defined by law as their property. Administering credit as a public utility should be a part of a fair democratic system.

Whether this will ever be done is irrelevant. The point is to understand the concept so we will not accept another Federal Reserve Central Bank hoax again!

-Part Four-

©

Flinchpaugh Gazette

August 16, 2011

Let the American People Benefit

Our country is bankrupt because of our out-of-control spending, financed not by transparent taxes, but by hidden continuous borrowing from the privately owned Federal Reserve banking cartel that charges us unnecessary interest for loaning us our own money.

High unemployment is not occurring because there is a shortage of jobs; but only a shortage of paper money to keep track of a person adding value to a product or service. Our country is blessed with abundant resources and intelligent, hardworking people who want to work and who are willing to work. There is just not enough paper money in circulation to make commerce operate efficiently. However, this money could be readily available, interest free and inflation free, from the U.S. Treasury Department, which can increase the money supply and not be inflationary as long as it does not exceed the GDP less the money already in circulation.

It has been estimated that there is $3.4 trillion in circulation and that our Gross Domestic Product is $14.2 trillion. In other words there is a "gap" of $10.8 trillion in purchasing power that must be filled by the American people by increased borrowing to be able to consume our GDP. This situation is highly profitable for the banks but disastrous for the American public.

Why not allow the people to benefit from this situation instead of the private banks? The solution to this inequity is a highly guarded secret. It is a monetary concept called, **"Credit as a Public Utility."** Instead of giving the Wall Street investment banks, (which should be located in the gambling city of Las Vegas), another stimulus, let's really stimulate our economy by giving the stimulus to every legal adult American. A few years ago the "gap" was estimated to be about $10,000 per person.

Let the American people who did the work benefit from the excess GDP instead of the banks who had nothing to do with the excess GDP.

𝕱𝖑𝖎𝖓𝖈𝖍𝖕𝖆𝖚𝖌𝖍 𝕲𝖆𝖟𝖊𝖙𝖙𝖊
November 10, 2008

Abolish the Fed" Now

The recent bail outs of the "fat cats" and bankers on Wall Street (with no benefit to the average citizen) approved by the leaders of both the Republican and Democrat parties should convince you that the Federal Reserve System must be abolished. Seeing what is happening on Wall Street, the real estate market, rising inflation and the financial problems of AIG, Bear Sterns, Lehman Brothers, etc. should tell you that something is seriously wrong with our monetary system.

When the unconstitutional Federal Reserve Act was passed in 1913, it was supposed to protect the American economy from recessions, inflation and depressions. It obviously is not working very well. In fact, the dollar has lost 95% of its value due to inflation since the "Fed" began. The "Banksters" cause the so called "business cycles" to the detriment of us citizens but to the enormous benefit of these banking insiders. Under their control, they make billions of dollars whether in good economic times or {especially} in "bad times." Abolishing the "Fed" is the most important step we can take towards solving our nations financial problems.

In 1913 Congress unconstitutionally gave a private bank control of our country's monetary system by enacting the Federal Reserve Act. This gave the bankers the authority to create and print "Fiat" money with no backing and loan it to the United States government and *charge it interest*. Most people do not know that the Federal Reserve is not Federal and it has no reserves. In fact it is listed next to "Federal Express" in the business white pages of most phone books.

Also in 1913, the Sixteenth Amendment was passed authorizing an income tax to be collected based upon people's wages. Our country had operated fine for over 125 years with no income tax. Most of this individual income tax you pay to the IRS does *not* go to run the country. It mostly goes to pay the Federal Reserve for interest it charges for loaning us our own money! If anyone else does this, it is called counterfeiting and extortion.

Just think how much you personally could stimulate the economy and how much your living standard would increase if you were not required to pay income tax on your wages.

Congress got us into this mess in 1913 and can get us out of it by repealing the Sixteenth Amendment and the Federal Reserve Act. An even easier way to abolish the "Fed" would be to have the president, by executive order, bypass the Federal Reserve and have the United States Treasury Department print *interest free* treasury notes. Since paper money doesn't last very long and needs to be replaced, in 2-3 years the Federal Reserve notes would no longer be in circulation and the unnecessary Federal Reserve would be out of business.

You hear very little from the politicians and the mainstream media about abolishing the Federal Reserve.

The unconstitutionality and the massive thievery by the unnecessary "Fed" has been one of the biggest secrets ever kept from the American people. These central bankers are so rich and powerful they literally control the Democrat and Republican Party and the mainstream media.

"It is well enough that the people of the nation do not understand our banking and monetary system, for if they did, I believe there would be a revolution before tomorrow morning."—
Henry Ford

"Let me issue and control a nation's money and I care not who writes the laws."—
Mayer Rothschild

"Most Americans have no real understanding of the operations of the international moneylenders...The accounts of the Federal Reserve have never been audited. It operates outside the control of Congress and...manipulates the credit of the United States."—
Senator Barry Goldwater

It is your duty and obligation as an American citizen to get informed and pressure our representatives to do what is in the best interest of the masses of the people; not just the elite bankers.

𝕱𝖑𝖎𝖓𝖈𝖍𝖕𝖆𝖚𝖌𝖍 𝕲𝖆𝖟𝖊𝖙𝖙𝖊
November 27, 2008

Averting a Financial Collapse

Many of those that read my earlier expose requesting the American voter to support the politicians that would abolish the Federal Reserve and income taxes on our salaries may think that this is an insane idea. I have had friends of mine say, "How would we pay for our schools, highways, and other government services?" What they don't realize is that the income tax collected on our wages goes mainly to pay for unnecessary interest the private Federal Reserve charges our government for loaning us **our own money**. Local county property taxes pays for our schools and the federal and state motor fuel tax pays for our highway system.

Ever since the Federal Reserve Act and the 16th Amendment authorizing tax on our salaries was passed in 1913, the entire world has had to suffer from this unconstitutional and evil act. The average person is not aware of the part played by our banking system in getting the United States involved in World War I and World War II. The international bankers, which include our Federal Reserve, supported a war against Germany and Japan. Germany in 1939 and Japan in 1942 had bypassed their private banks and adopted a money system where the **state** created the money supply at **zero interest.** The international bankers were terrified that other countries would replicate this superior banking system which does not siphon off unnecessary money from the citizens. This was a serious threat to the private investors of the United States Federal Reserve and a world war would be one way of countering it. Of course this is not the only cause of World War II, but *the banking issue isn't even discussed as one cause for the war.*

Just think how much you personally could stimulate the economy and how much your living standard would improve if you were not required to pay income tax on your salary. This tax is in fact a form of slavery because you are required to work a portion of your day with no pay.

It is very disheartening to see that none of our elected politicians (except Ron Paul) or news media celebrities even discusses this issue. The American people have not been given the facts about our current monetary system. Maybe if more people would seriously investigate the Federal Reserve's short comings, we could make the necessary changes to save our country from a financial collapse.

𝕱lincfpaugf Gazette
February 20, 2009

Economic Stimulus Bailout

A couple of weeks ago, a TV news reporter asked his guest if they believed the "Economic Stimulus" plan was going to work. The guest said, "Absolutely." "It will increase the debt and will increase the size of our government." I thought, "Wow, this guy hit the nail on the head." Not expecting such an honest answer the reporter immediately switched to another subject. Why won't the controlled mainstream media and our elected representatives discuss what really needs to be done to fix our economic problems; abolish the private *Federal Reserve* and *Fractional Reserve Banking*?

Just a few months ago we were arguing the merits of passing a bailout stimulus package. At that time the only ones who approved of the bailouts were the Investment Bankers and their congressional cronies, Nancy Pelosi, Harry Reid and both presidential candidates. It didn't seem to matter that millions of American citizens' did not support the bailout.

Why would anyone in their right mind support bailing out those companies that made very poor management decisions with some even engaged in criminal activity plus paying their executives enormous salaries and bonuses as they were going broke. Bailing out these companies is no different than bailing out Las Vegas gamblers. Today the propaganda machine has convinced most of the "sheeple" that it was necessary and the right thing to do. Many people seem to believe that it is the federal government's responsibility to solve all of our problems by redistributing the wealth. This kind of reasoning will eventually cause our whole system to collapse. We will never get out of debt and solve our economic problems until the private *Federal Reserve* and *Fractional Reserve Banking* are abolished.

The bailout stimulus package is doing the same thing that got us into this mess in the first place; devaluating our existing dollars by printing more and more fiat money to finance the bailout of banksters and connected corporate cronies.

Our present *deplorable* economic status is probably normal considering our government's failed monetary policies. What we thought was normal earlier when our government and economy *appeared* to be in good shape was in fact only a fragile propped up house of cards based on our government's polices of unlimited credit for everyone.

𝔉lintfpaugh 𝔊a𝔷ette
March 21, 2012

Eggs and Issues" Breakfast

Wednesday morning, March 21, the President of the Kansas City Federal Reserve made a talk at Missouri Western University "Eggs and Issues" breakfast. Mrs. George, a Missouri Western Alumnus, gave an interesting commentary about the history of the Federal Reserve and our current economic situation. It is not every day that someone of this importance comes to St. Joseph giving us the opportunity to get firsthand information concerning the Federal Reserve which contrary to popular belief is not **"Federal"** and has no **"Reserves."**

I have been writing about the Federal Reserve and Fractional Reserve Banking now for over six years and have written numerous Letters to the Editor to both the "Telegraph" and the St. Joseph "News Press." Additionally, I have written a book on the subject, "Secrets of Our Hidden Controllers Revealed" which is available on Amazon.com, Hastings and the St. Joseph libraries. My main agenda has been to convince the reader the importance of abolishing the private Federal Reserve Bank and Fractional Reserve Banking for our local banks unless they are owned by the state of Missouri.

There was only enough time allocated for three of the attendees to ask questions. Not wanting to miss this opportunity, I immediately stood up when she opened the floor to questions. Actually I squeezed in two questions:

(1) I asked, "Out of the 15 trillion dollar American debt, how much of that is owed to the private Federal Reserve? I have read that it is nearly 50% or 6-7 trillion dollars but would like to have that figure verified."

Her answer didn't confirm nor deny the 6-7 trillion dollar amount that I had received from what I believe to be a reliable source. She did say something about three trillion dollars. I would guess that her figure is lower because of the way the intergovernmental expenses are tabulated. In any event we didn't have time to discuss the discrepancy.

(2) Then I asked, "Since 1913 we have allowed the Federal Reserve to print our money supply and charge the American tax payer interest for loaning us our own money. Why would we do this when the U.S. Treasury Department can print our money supply interest free, and is authorized by the Constitution?" Then I added that the usual answer to this question is that you can't trust the politicians to handle our money without causing inflation or a depression because they will print an excessive amount of money to cover their out of control spending. I explained that Congress could not have done any worse than the Federal Reserve since the Federal Reserve was not able to prevent the 1929 depression or the numerous recessions and booms and bust business cycles. I also pointed out that since the Federal Reserve Act was passed in 1913, the purchasing value of the dollar has dropped by more than 90%. Prices of consumer goods and services are going up because the purchasing power of the dollar is going down.

Again, her answer didn't adequately address the question.

Abolishing the private Federal Reserve could be easier than most people realize. Forget trying to amend the Constitution or getting Congress to help. The President could, by executive order, have the U.S. Treasury Department print our money *as interest free Treasury notes* instead of *Interest bearing Federal*

Reserve notes. Due to the short life cycle of paper money, there would be no Federal Reserve notes left in a very short time. President Kennedy actually did this but was tragically assassinated just three months later. Our new president, President Johnson, immediately recalled the Treasury notes and had them destroyed.

The main argument for abolishing the Fed is that we would no longer be required to pay an unconstitutional income tax on our citizens' salaries. Ronald Reagan did a study that showed that income tax on our salaries went to pay the Federal Reserve the interest they charge the taxpayer and not for any governmental services.

Another benefit that you rarely hear is that if the Federal Reserve was abolished, the likelihood of war would be greatly diminished. Currently our continuous offensive wars are financed through *debt financing* from borrowing from outside sources or borrowing from the Fed and paying huge amounts of interest in both cases. This

means the taxpayer is paying for the wars through the hidden inflation tax. Just imagine if the wars could no longer be financed through this **hidden** tax and had to be paid for through an increase in your **transparent** income tax. The President might come on the nightly news and explain that the U.S. was going to attack a country but didn't have the money for a war. And since it could no longer be borrowed our income tax rate would have to go up 30 or 40%. He might say, "I hope you folks don't mind." Do you really think the public would accept this?

Closely related to the *Federal Reserve* issue is *Fractional Reserve Banking.* If Missouri allowed Fractional Reserve Banking for only a state owned bank, the profit generated would go to the taxpayer instead of a private bank. This would allow the state, counties, and cities the opportunity to finance public works projects like new sewers for St. Joe interest free. Private Banks would still exist but could only loan out their own money.

Having a sound monetary system at both the Federal level and State level is the key to solving our major problems including the creation of jobs, an increase in the quality of life where you have enough income to purchase your own health care insurance, and the reduction of war.

Let's make the changes now while we are still fairly well fed and housed. If we wait until our economy collapses, we will be forced to accept whatever the elite bankers propose, and I guarantee it will not be in the best interest of the American people. But by that time we will be too cold and hungry to resist.

𝔉𝔩𝔦𝔫𝔠𝔥𝔭𝔞𝔲𝔤𝔥 𝔊𝔞𝔷𝔢𝔱𝔱𝔢
April 7, 2010

No Shortage of Jobs

No matter what you have been told, there is **not** a shortage of jobs. Each of us needs food, shelter, clothing, utilities, transportation and healthcare and most of us are willing to work for it. This country is still rich in natural resources, innovation and people who are eager to work. The problem is that there is not enough money to keep track of the effort each of us expends in adding value to a product or service.

Look at the depression in the 1930's where we had 25% unemployment and farm prices fell by 60%. The unemployment figures showed that there was not enough money to pay employees; not that there were people unwilling to work. There was a *contrived* shortage of money and banks foreclosed on millions of our citizens' homes, farms and businesses. But, as soon as the bankers decided that we had to go to war, there was plenty of money for tanks, airplanes, etc.

One of the most important jobs of our government is to have a monetary system that serves the people instead of the bankers. There is a simple but little understood solution, that even most of our *elected leaders* don't understand. The *unelected leaders* understand but keep it a secret.

We must abolish (1) the privately owned Federal Reserve banking cartel that charges us interest for loaning us our own money and then allow our Treasury department to print our money interest free, (2) Fractional Reserve banking where a bank can loan up to 90% of their depositors' money and (3) income tax on our citizens' salary.

A rather radical and revolutionary idea would be for our country to declare bankruptcy and write off the estimated 11% to 45% of our nation's debt that is "owed"

to the private Federal Reserve. Note: *Kansas City Fed President claims it is about 24%.*

You need not feel sorry for the banksters because they have stolen many times this amount from the American tax payer since the enactment in 1913 of the Federal Reserve Act and the 16th Amendment.

Don't be concerned about inflation with the U.S. Treasury Department printing our money. It couldn't be any worse than the Federal Reserve's record where our dollar has lost 95% of its value since 1913.

It is only going to get worse with the bailouts of our banks and companies that are "Too Big to Fail." We are rewarding these companies for their inefficient activities and sometime criminal behavior at tax payers' expense.

Flinchpaugh Gazette
May 12, 2011

The Ultimate Solution

Let's face it. Our country is in a financial crisis and few of our leaders know what to do. Those few who do know are unfairly marginalized by being labeled far right extremists. However, they only appear to be far right because there are so many that are so far left.

Not only is our country bankrupt, it is broken in so many other ways; (1) a large majority of our politicians do not honor their oath to uphold the Constitution when voting for legislation, (2) our presidents continue to abuse executive orders to go to war without approval from Congress which has done nothing but create more terrorists and huge profits for the bankers and military industrial complex companies, (3) state sovereignty is completely ignored when the Federal Government sues a state like Arizona claiming their immigration policies violate federal law. This practice will most likely continue with the Federal government suing those states who voted to exempt their state from the unconstitutional federal healthcare mandates, (4) the Commerce Clause in our Constitution is mis-interpreted by Washington to justify almost any action they claim is in the best interest of the people and (5) starting in 1993, there has been a huge increase in questionable "Over the Counter" (OTC) derivatives, which has been estimated to be over a hundred trillion dollars annually. These investments were virtually ignored by the regulators which allowed companies like Enron to be exempt from regulation in the trading of derivatives. The economic losses to investors have been astronomical.

We are not even able to solve our 1.6 trillion dollar

75

deficit for the year 2011. The republican leadership is so proud to get a measly 38 billion dollar spending cut that does nothing but insult the intelligence of the electorate. That is only a 2.4% cut. (38 billion/1600 billion = 2.4%). Many of the legislators, including President Obama, keep trying to scare the public and hide the obvious by claiming that we must tax the rich in addition to cutting expenses like Medicare and Social Security. As Senator Rand Paul so astutely notes, "We don't have a tax problem, we have a spending problem."

What is truly ironic is that our economy today is exactly where it should be considering our flawed banking system and financial policies. What we thought was a booming healthy economy a few years ago was a facade. It was based on (1) a dollar that was being propped up by most of the world trading oil in American dollars (2) a phony corrupt home loan program at Fanny Mae and Freddie Mac that made loans to people that they knew would eventually default and (3)

cheap Chinese consumer goods that only make it appear that we are well off.

One immediate solution to our country's economic problems is to abolish the private "Federal Reserve System," that charges the taxpayers interest for loaning us our own money. We should write off the trillions of dollars owed them. No need to feel sorry for them, they have stolen way more than this from the American taxpayer since 1913. The U.S. Treasury Department can print our money 'Interest Free" and it is constitutional. Ron Paul and Dennis Kucinich are the only brave politicians who even talk about this and until just recently, the only political pundit to suggest that the Federal Reserve just might be the cause of our problems is Glen Beck.

The Federal Reserve Act has failed miserably in eliminating the boom and bust business cycles caused by inflation and poor financial management.

Abolishing the private Federal Reserve is the most important issue you will ever consider, followed closely by drastically curtailing our governments out of control spending to solve our country's economic problems. Every one of us need to diligently study these issues so we can intelligently vote for those legislators who will make the necessary changes to return our country to that which was envisioned by our founding fathers.

Flinchpaugh Gazette
April 4, 2011

Budget Crisis

Our congressmen still don't get it and will pay a heavy price in the coming elections unless they start representing their constituents instead of the special interest groups. The Tea Party groups, with the support of a substantial number of American citizens, has demanded that we have a balanced budget and through the election process is replacing those politicians who are not representing them.

Both the Democrats and the Republicans are now arguing about cutting 30 to 60 billion dollars from a budget *deficit* of 1.6 trillion. (1600 billion) Thirty billion dollars is only a 2% cut which is meaningless plus it is an insult to the intelligence of the American people. Instead of solving only 2% of the budget crisis (30/1600=2%), why not cut 1600 billion dollars in expenses so we can have a 100% balanced budget. Problem solved!

Don't let the political fear mongers scare you by saying the cuts will have to come from Social Security and Medicare. That's just not true. There are billions of dollars that can be cut by abolishing, but not limited to, the Patriot Act, Federal Department of Education, Energy Department, Housing and Urban Development, Farm Subsidies, and financial and military aid to all countries including Israel. Most of these are unconstitutional anyway; as if that makes any difference.

Billions more could be saved by decriminalizing drug use and by treating drug addicts as sick people instead of making them into criminals. Not only would we save the cost of apprehension, prosecution and incarceration but we could collect billions in taxes on the drugs. No, I don't condone the use of illegal addictive drugs but it should be clear to everyone that the "War on Drugs" isn't working and never will.

Also we can declare our country bankrupt and write off the 48% owed to the privately owned Federal Reserve who charges us interest for printing and loaning us our own money. *Note: Kansas City Fed President claims it is about* *24%.* (48% of our 14 trillion dollar debt is 6.72 trillion dollars) Not only would that allow us to balance our budget but it would also pay off almost one half of our national debt.

No need to feel sorry for the bankers because they have stolen much more than the 6.7 trillion dollars from the American tax payer since 1913 when the unconstitutional Federal Reserve Act and the 16th Amendment were passed. The 16th Amendment allowed the government to collect income tax on its citizen's salaries which goes mainly to pay the Federal Reserve interest rather than any government services for the people.

Flinchpaugh Gazette
May 6, 2010

Who are the Real Patriots?

Just who are the real patriots anyway? It certainly is not the majority of our elected leaders who fail to honor the oath to the Constitution they swore to uphold and think the Constitution is an outdated relic of the past.

There are a higher percentage of true patriots involved in political activist groups like "Campaign for Liberty", the various "Tea

78

Party" groups, "Oath Keepers" and the "John Birch Society" than in our country's leaders and the controlled mainstream media.

What's wrong with (1) demanding that our government abide by the Constitution and Bill of Rights, (2) demanding that we adopt sound monetary policies including the abolishment of the private Federal Reserve Banking cartel, (3) stop acting as the policeman of the world and (4) respecting the sovereignty of the states and an individual's liberty?

Why shouldn't we question the 9-11 attacks, the Kennedy Assassination, the OKC bombing, the Branch Dividian compound attack, the 1967 Israeli attack on an American ship (USS Liberty) that killed 34 American sailors etc.? It's not like we have been told the truth in the past. i.e.; Gulf of Tonkin, weapons of mass destruction, global warming hoax, and the exaggerated Russian cold war threat hoax.

By today's standards of the controlling elite and the dummied down electorate, George Washington, Thomas Jefferson and Benjamin Franklin would be labeled as unpatriotic and suspected terrorists.

Be wary of those labeling the true patriots as Anti-Semitic, conspiracy nuts, paranoid, truthers, birthers, right winger, etc. It just may be that those doing the labeling are the real threat and are the most unpatriotic because of their attempt to marginalize the true patriots.

Flinchpaugh Gazette
July 23, 2011

To ALL SPECIAL INTEREST GROUPS
Including
The International Bankers, the Military Industrial Complex Companies and the Israeli Lobby

I think it is time for you to thank American's brave men and women in our armed forces that have so valiantly protected your interests. The U.S. military continues to wage, *offensive* rather than *defensive,* undeclared wars throughout the world on your behalf that have not been approved by the majority of the United States Congress or the American people.

Be ever mindful of the billions of dollars in profits that our armed forces have made possible for you power hungry profiteers in the guise of protecting America from the so called terrorists which our flawed foreign policy has created. We put our soldiers on the battle field, with many losing their lives or being physical or mentally crippled for life, not to defend America, but rather to protect your selfish interests.

It is time for you profiteers and power hungry world leaders to be stopped and allow the United States to return to a country that abides by its constitution and respects the sovereignty of all foreign countries including the individual states within these *united states*.

Not only can we not afford to continue being the "policeman" of the world, it is immoral for a powerful civilized country like the U.S. to continually interfere in the lives of people in other countries. Our interference has resulted in unnecessary suffering for both civilians and soldiers. Our country's foreign policies must be that of a responsible civilized society that represents the interest of the people instead of you special interest groups whose main agenda is profit and power with no thought given to using our brave soldiers as cannon fodder.

𝔉𝔩𝔦𝔫𝔠𝔥𝔭𝔞𝔲𝔤𝔥 𝔊𝔞𝔷𝔢𝔱𝔱𝔢
December 10, 2012

How To Pay Off the National Debt

Neither the Democrats nor the Republicans have any intention of paying off the national debt. It is politically more beneficial for the politicians to finance their excessive spending through hidden *debt financing* rather than through *transparent taxes.* Financing our government through transparent taxes, would immediately inform the taxpayer of the folly of the politicians excessive spending because of extremely higher personal income tax. This would most definitely assure the politicians of being elected for only one term.

Even if our government's leaders wanted to pay off the $16 trillion dollar debt, it is not possible under our current banking system. Our economy (money supply) is always short the amount of interest that *was not* created through fractional reserve banking. When the bank approves your loan, they create the principal out of thin air but the interest is not created at all. The Federal Government will have to create this money by borrowing it from the privately owned Federal Reserve Bank which charges the taxpayers interest. The interest, not created by the Federal Reserve's loan, forces our government to borrow even more money. It is a never ending cycle; the federal debt can never be paid off.

The only solution is to:

- Abolish the ***unconstitutional Federal Reserve*** and allow the U.S. Treasury Department to issue our money supply interest free, as provided for in the Constitution. This won't be inflationary as long as they don't issue more than the difference between the total GDP less the money already in circulation. In other words, there is not enough money in circulation to conduct commerce in a way as to consume the excess production. In order for the people to consume this excess production, they could purchase it by charging it to their credit card, which is done now, or the Federal Government could give all Americans a stimulus check instead of allowing the banks to profit for something they had nothing to do with. This concept is referred to as ***Credit as a Public Utility***. Even if you think this is an unrealistic idea, and is unlikely to be adopted, it still helps to explain our flawed and unconstitutional banking system.
- Allow ***fractional reserve banking*** for only those banks owned by the state (North Dakota is currently the only state with a state owned bank). Instead of private banks

profiting from fractional reserve banking, the taxpayers would profit. This profit could then pay for many of the state's public works projects, *interest free.*
- The Federal Government should declare bankruptcy and write off the $4 trillion or so owed the privately owned Federal Reserve. Don't feel sorry for them. They have stolen much more than that from the American people since 1913. (Write off just the amount owed to the Fed and any other banks in the world that are affiliated with them; not individual bond holders.)
- The next step is to finance the operation of our government only through **transparent taxes** instead of through **non-transparent** debt financing. Debt financing should only be used in extreme emergencies, like when another country invades the U.S. or a meteor hits the U.S. and destroys huge areas of the country. Everything else must be paid for thru taxation. Debt financing taxes the people twice; a hidden inflation tax plus the normal income tax.

A side benefit to my proposal, besides paying off the national debt, would be that it would almost eliminate all wars or *Regime change*, as some refer to it. Just imagine the President appearing on the six o'clock news and saying, "My fellow Americans, the United Nations, not Congress, has advised me that the U.S. must nuke Iceland because they won't allow us to steal their oil or allow the international bankers to take over their banking system. Since we can no longer resort to hidden *debt financing,* we are going to increase your income tax for the next five years, 40%."

What do you think would happen? We definitely would not go to war and the President would probably be impeached; it surely would be the end of his political career.

We continuously vote every four years for both Republican and Democrat leaders that represent the *Banksters* instead of the people. Nothing much will change, until the public understands that our current banking system is unconstitutional and that the Federal Reserve Bank is privately owned, created for the sole purpose of making huge profits for themselves at the expense of the American people.

Revolutionary but Necessary Solution

Let's face it, our country is bankrupt. If our government devalues the dollar 50% or more it will be devastating to our economy and way of life. There would be a monumental increase in real estate foreclosures, bankruptcies and crime. Out of desperation, normally honest people would resort to whatever it took to feed and clothe their family. Even an honest person will steal for food if they go without it for a few days and soon thereafter will maybe even kill for food.

There is a solution. The American people should demand that our government declare bankruptcy and write off the 48% of the national debt owed to the private Federal Reserve banking cartel. (.48 x 14 trillion = 6.7 trillion dollars) Additionally the government could insist that all governmental agencies cut their budget by 10%. No need to feel sorry for the bankers; they have stolen many times this 6.7 trillion dollars from the American people since 1913 when the Federal Reserve Act was fraudulently passed.

This unconstitutional banking system that prints our money (Federal Reserve Notes) and charges us interest should be replaced with the United States Treasury printing our money supply "Interest Free." Why in the world would we have a monetary system that requires us to pay unnecessary interest? Even worse is that the 16th Amendment, also passed in 1913, allows the federal government to charge income tax on its citizen's salaries; not for government services but to pay the interest. The banking interests are so powerful, writing your congressman will most likely not make any difference. Lets hope and pray that the needed changes can be accomplished peaceably.

Liberty? or Tyranny?

Together we can return our country to that which was envisioned by our founding fathers.

What do **true** Patriots stand for?
A government that:

- *Abides by the Constitution.*
- *Adopts sound monetary policies by abolishing the privately owned **Federal Reserve**, **Fractional Reserve Banking** and **Income Tax** on the citizen's salaries.*
- *Stops trying to be the policeman of the world.*
- *Recognizes the sovereignty of the individual states and*
- *each citizens liberty.*

Make your vote count. Vote for only those legislators that score 50% or higher on the Constitutional scorecard. Google *The Freedom Index* for a list of your representative's voting record concerning Constitutional issues

Recommend Reading:
Secrets of our Hidden Controllers Revealed by: Larry
Flinchpaugh --$15.00 at Amazon.com books.

This book discusses how our opinions have been distorted by government propaganda, the controlled mainstream news media, our educational system and our religious leaders. It also discusses what you as an individual can do to help solve our economic issues and return our government to that which our founding fathers intended.

Against All Odds-President Paul Rronan
By: Larry Flinchpaugh

This exciting Historical Novel follows the lives of four members of the Ronan family, from 1859-2012, as they influence the American political system to once again establish a Constitutional Republic from a failed Democracy.

The Creature from Jekyll Island- A Second Look at the Federal Reserve
By G. Edward Griffin

This is an excellent book about the origins of the Federal Reserve

The Web of Debt by Ellen Hodgson Brown, J.D.

Ellen Hodgson Brown, author of the book, "The Web of Debt" explains the shocking truth about our money system and how we can break free and why paper money does not need to be backed by gold. She makes it very clear that if the United States issued its own money, that money could cover all of its expenses, and the income tax would not be needed.

She explains how Adolph Hitler got Germany out of a severe depression when he came to power in 1933. Germany's economy was in total disarray because of ruinous World War 1 war-reparation obligations and he was unable to get foreign investments or credit from the **international bankers**. By printing his own debt free paper money, in four years, he was able to develop Germany into the strongest economy in Europe. Hitler was able to finance Germany's entire government and war effort from 1935 to 1945 without gold or debt from the private banks.

The international bankers felt they had to put a stop to Hitler before he influenced other countries by showing them how successful they could be by printing their own debt free money without any gold or silver backing. Ellen Hodgson Brown says in her book, *"....and it took the whole Capitalist and Communist world to destroy the German power over Europe and bring Europe back under the heel of the bankers. Such history of money does not appear in the textbooks of public (government) schools today."*

Recommended Web Sites:

Alex Jones' www.infowars.com

G. Edward Griffin www.gedwardgriffin.com

(RBN) The Republic Broadcasting Network
www.republicbroadcasting.org

Lew Rockwell www.lewrockwell.com

Recommended Newspaper:

"The American Free Press."
645 Pennsylvania Avenue SE, Suite 100
Washington, D.C. 20003
1-888-699-6397 or www.americanfreepress.net

Recommended documentaries:
The Obama Deception by Alex Jones
America: Freedom to Fascism by Aaron Russo
Zeitgeist, the Movie by Peter Joseph
The Money Masters
Fall of the Republic by Alex Jones
Loose Change Final Cut
Secrets of Oz

Recommended Political Activist Groups:

Tea Party Groups (Those supporting Ron Paul's Platform)

Campaign for Liberty: www.campaignforliberty.com

Restore the Republic: www.restoretherepublic.com

Additional Publications by
J L Flinchpaugh Publishing Company
St. Joseph, Missouri

www.amazon.com/books
lflinch@stjoelive.com
www.larryflinchpaugh.com

Secrets of Our Hidden Controllers Revealed

November 1, 2009

$15.00

Discover how the unelected controllers of our government control our lives and dictate what we do and think. I dare you to read this book. If it doesn't irritate you, I haven't accomplished my objective to get your attention. Unfortunately, most people are simply too apathetic and too busy to get involved with new thoughts and ideas that would drastically change their **outdated** opinions.

Most of the information presented in this book will more than likely be outside your *comfort zone.*

Perhaps you think you already know all you need to know about religion and the important political issues facing us today.

The ideas presented in this book may be shocking-but I sincerely hope it will open your eyes and expand your mind. This is more important than agreeing with the author on every issue.

BILLION$ FOR THE BANKER$
Debts For The People
June 2009
$5.00

 This 1984 informative reprint of Sheldon Emry's booklet will give the reader greater insight into our country's monetary system and explains why we must abolish the privately owned Federal Reserve Banking cartel that has, from 1913, been in charge of printing our money and loaning it to the American government with interest. The U.S. Treasury Department can print our money "Interest Free," making it unnecessary to pay income tax on our citizen's wages.

Sheldon Emry's original book was not copyrighted and neither is the reprinted portion. The publisher, Larry Flinchpaugh, has added two extra copyrighted sections to help bring the booklet up to date a bit. Even though some of the information is a little outdated it is still relevant today.

Contrary to popular belief, the only reason our paper money should be backed by gold and silver is because that is what is required by the Constitution. Paper money is only a means to account for the value a person adds to the economy through his labor, investment and risk. That plus the government's willingness to accept it as payment of taxes is the only backing it needs.

It is imperative that the public understands are current flawed monetary system so that they will not be tricked into another Federal Reserve type deception when our economic system finally collapses.

Consider purchasing several of these booklets at this low price and give them to your friends and legislators.

Growing Up In a Zoo
February 2011
$15.00

This is a story of Larry Flinchpaugh growing up in St. Joseph, Missouri in the 1940's through the 1960's and working in his parents Pet Shop, Zoo, and Reptile Gardens. The facility was located at 3727 Frederick Avenue-old highway 36. (Now the home of The Citizens Bank and Trust Company)

The book is full of interesting and amusing stories regarding his experience in training and handling their pet chimpanzee, Vicky Lynn. Vicky not only appeared regularly at the Krug Park Bowl, KFEQ TV, daily shows at the Zoo but even had a part in a Harvard Biology training film. Other stories include the part Larry played in the heroic Air Force flight from Homestead Air force base in Florida to Rosecrans Field in St. Joe. That flight saved the life of one of the Zoo's employees, Bill White, after he had been bitten by an Indian cobra. This story was carried by almost every major news outlet throughout the world.

There are many pictures and interesting stories included which should be of special interest to those who came from miles around to tour the facility and to be entertained and educated about a wide variety of animals, birds and reptiles. Even those people who never toured the Zoo but love animals and animal stories will find the stories entertaining and educational.

Vicky was one of the Flinchpaugh family Members. She ate with them in their private kitchen at the zoo facility but had her own sleeping cage. It was very sad when she reached the age of about eight and began to rebel; just like us humans.

Against All Odds
President Paul Ronan
$15.00

This exciting story follows the lives of four members of the Ronan family, from 1859-2012, as they influence the American political system to once again establish a Constitutional Republic.

In 1859, the protagonist, Sam Ronan comes to America from Ireland and becomes a telegraph operator in Philadelphia and shortly thereafter, he gets a job in *Breckenridge, Missouri* as a telegrapher for the *Hannibal and St. Joseph Railroad.*

Because the *Confederate bushwhackers* had sabotaged the bridge over the *Platt River,* Sam almost loses his life while traveling to St. Joe on the train. Having graduated from Harvard, magna cum laude, Sam's son Jeff lands a job working for President Woodrow Wilson in Washington, D.C.

Matt, Sam's grandson, meets the love of his life at the *Frog Hop Ball Room* in St. Joseph and becomes a successful farmer and Federal Congressman.

Graduating from *Central High School* in St. Joseph, Mo., Sam's great-grandson, Paul, obtains a medical degree from Baylor University in Texas and then joins the Navy and nearly loses his life when the Israelis attacked his reconnaissance ship, the *USS Liberty in 1967.* Honorably discharged from the Navy, Paul becomes a Texas Congressman and after a ruthless campaign in 2012, he is overwhelmingly *elected President of the United States.*

Each one of the four generations of the Ronan family added greatly to the security and financial wellbeing of this country's citizens. You will learn how Paul Ronan obtained full employment, truly "affordable" health care, a balanced budget, a plan to totally "pay off" the national debt, all in a candid *entertaining and educational story format.*

Letters Home From Civil War Soldier Charles W. Gamble
(1862-1864)
Compiled by Mark Flinchpaugh, April 2011.

$15.00

These historic letters included in this book were written in the 1860's by Union soldier, Charles W. Gamble, to his wife and family during the Civil War. He bravely served with the 12th regiment, New Jersey volunteers, Company D. A carpenter by trade, Charles joined the Union Army in August, 1862, "to as he stated, preserve the country and the Constitution." ***Note: Not to free the slaves.*** Several times in his letters he frankly wrote that he might not come back home alive, but he was serving for a just cause. This is a fascinating and personal account of a common soldier's life serving his country and fighting to keep the Union intact. Told from the intimate perspective of a typical volunteer soldier, you will glean interesting tidbits of historical information not usually found in books about the Civil War.

You will come to feel that you know Charles personally as you read his actual letters about his daily activities during the war. From mundane chores to the horrors of battle at Gettysburg, you will experience Civil War life through Charles' own words.

No matter how difficult the hardships became Charles courageously pressed on for the good of the country. History comes alive in these insightful, heartwarming letters written nearly one hundred fifty years ago by Charles W. Gamble.

This book is available on Amazon.com and at all the St. Joseph libraries, book stores, most local museums and various tourist locations.

Should I Start
My Own
Business ?

January 20, 2013

$12.00

This self-help 127 page paperback book follows the various business ventures that Larry Flinchpaugh has been involved in from 1963 to 2005.

It starts out by asking the question, "Why do you want to start your own business?" Sadly many people start a business for the wrong reasons and many lose a good portion of their life savings in the first year or two.

The book explains how to write a **"Business Plan"** and prepare a **"Break Even Analysis"** to help the reader predict their chance of success or failure.

Although, not intended to be an accounting book, it does explain basic accounting functions, how to calculate an individual's **"Net Worth"** and how to prepare a "Balance Sheet" and "Profit and Loss" statement.

This book is available at Hastings on the Belt Highway in St. Joseph, Missouri, Amazon.com/books and all St. Joseph, Missouri libraries. It can also be obtained at most local libraries thru their inter-library loan program.

Movie Documentary
"This Is Our Town, St. Joseph, Missouri"
(Short preview is on YouTube)
$20.00

Filmed c. 1954. This movie was originally produced by "Robert M. Carson" productions on a 16MM film that was used as a promotional film for the city of St. Joe. It features several prominent businesses in St. Joe in the 1950's and shows nostalgic street scenes in a much different time.

The 16MM film was purchased by Mr. Flinchpaugh several years ago at a local estate sale from a former film collector. After retiring, Mr. Flinchpaugh re-discovered the long forgotten film in a box in his garage but noticed it had a strong odor smelling like bleach emitting from the metal film container. A quick check with "Accent Video" in Overland Park, Kansas confirmed that the film was rapidly deteriorating and needed to be restored immediately before it was entirely lost.

The film has been shown several times at the local libraries and civic organizations but anyone wishing to purchase a copy of the film may buy one at "Hastings" most of the local museums, the "St. Joseph Visitor Center" and Hy-Vee on the Belt highway.

Specific viewings for local civic groups, churches, and other clubs and organization can still be arranged by calling Larry at 816-676-2565 or email him at lflinch@stjoelive.com.

7850330R00057

Printed in Great Britain
by Amazon.co.uk, Ltd.,
Marston Gate.